RACE DAY

RACE DAY

A Spot on the Rail with

MAX WATMAN

IVAN R. DEE

Chicago 2005

www.ivanrdee.com

PHOTO CREDITS: pages 23, 103, 116: © Bettmann/CORBIS; page 33: © Pugilistica.com; page 45: Keeneland Library, Lexington, Ky.; pages 53, 67: *Louisville Courier-Journal*; page 72: © Kevin R. Morris/CORBIS; page 76: © Bob Krist/CORBIS; page 105: © Vince Streano/CORBIS; pages 128, 153, 181: © California Thoroughbred Breeders Association; page 137: © Marc Asnin/CORBIS; pages 157, 229: Max Watman; page 201: © Associated Press/Equi-Photo, Bill Denver; page 216: © Mike Seger/Reuters/CORBIS; page 224: Maryland Jockey Club.

Library of Congress Cataloging-in-Publication Data:
Watman, Max.
  Race day : a spot on the rail with Max Watman / Max Watman.
    p. cm.
  Includes index.
  ISBN 1-56663-608-6 (cloth : alk. paper)
  1. Horse racing—United States—Anecdotes. 2. Race horses—United States—Anecdotes. 3. Horsemen and horsewomen—United States—Anecdotes. 4. Watman, Max. I. Title.
  SF335.5.W38 2005
  798.4'00973—dc22   2005005375

For Pops the tout

Contents

Preface

OUR UNREMITTING recording of race results has created an immense archival narrative of speed. Racehorses are all about speed—distance measured by time. A racehorse runs one length in about one-fifth of a second.* There are 480 lengths—480 fifths of a second—to the mile. Each mile is recorded, so all that speed has been recorded over time to create history.

Horse races are short—two and a half minutes tops. Before the horses break, the race is potential and possibility. Races begin in mystery and probability: the horses are being loaded into the gate, in moments the gate will open and the race will culminate in a rush of excitement. A hundred and twenty seconds later, possibility will have metamorphosed into truth, fiction into fact, suspicion into realization.

I have on my desk a results chart for Man o' War's Preakness in 1920. It looks no different from yesterday's charts.

*Some argue that it's actually one-quarter of a second, but historically racing times have been measured in fifths of a second, and it's easier just to play along.

Charts are the barest record of horse racing, but they are wildly suggestive. Embedded in the names of the jockeys, trainers, and owners, in the place names and the dates, are stories. Some of these tales are well known, some aren't. Some have implications, others don't.

I've thought of this book as a perfect day at the races, picked a handful of my favorite anecdotes, and strung them together. There will be triumphs and upsets. Dead cert chalk will run against outmatched plodders. Dreams will be realized and smashed. If you flipped through all the records and picked out every race on the card for a day that would evoke the maximum pathos and suss out a story about America and American racing and the places and people who made it, you would undoubtedly come up with a different set. But these are good stories.

George Plimpton's famous interview with Ernest Hemingway was the twenty-first in the *Paris Review's* series titled "The Art of Fiction." It begins,

> HEMINGWAY: You go to the races?
>
> INTERVIEWER: Yes, occasionally.
>
> HEMINGWAY: Then you read the *Racing Form* . . . there you have the true Art of Fiction.

Probably more a complaint about a bad day at the track than any kind of deep insight.

Yet there's truth there. A day at the track is a day spent creating stories out of the numbers and short descriptive clauses that summarize the performances of horses. "Much the best . . . won driving . . . improved position while failing to

threaten . . . handily . . . willing third . . . no final response
. . . lugged out, weakened . . . vied, cleared, got nod." There
in the *Form*, too, are the times of each piece of the race. They
give you the pace, the quickness with which the race started,
the vigor or apathy with which it was won. You look at the
breeding, you look at the trainer, you look at the jockey, and
you swirl all of it together to create a fiction of how the race
will be run. You make your choice, you place your bet. You've
told yourself a story, and you hope that your story goes down
in history with all the others. It happens all day, every day, two
minutes at a time. A race is run, someone was right, and that
story is the one that went down in the books. More than the
money, that's what you're cheering home. When the horses hit
the stretch, everyone is trying to break even in the biggest possible way. You asserted your imagination, looked at the world,
and predicted its course. You want your version to be true.

Enjoy the races. Good luck.

Acknowledgments

THANKS TO Ivan Dee for inviting me to write this book.

For your generous help: Alan Carter, Dick Hamilton, and Tom Gilcoyne at the National Thoroughbred Racing Museum and Hall of Fame; Phyllis Rogers and Cathy Schenck at the Keeneland library; Debra Ginsburg and Vivian Montoya at the California Thoroughbred Breeders Association.

Thanks to Richard and Rocio Ash, Bill Christine, John Crotty, Marcia and Joan Farrell, Brian Flynn, Allen Gutterman, Richard Holland, Lisa Jackson, Roger Kimball, Joanie Lawrence, Dan Leary, Dan Smith, Bill Thayer, the Thomas family, R. James Williams, and Mike Woodsworth.

Thanks to Neil Azevedo and Robert Messenger for their sharp minds and good advice.

Will and Carole Watman not only for their help with *Race Day* but for bringing me to my first race day.

Acknowledgments

Thanks to Rachael—*sine qua non*—for her generous agreement to spend her free time at the races and her careful reading of every word. She makes everything worthwhile and fun.

M. W.

Cold Spring, New York
March 2005

RACE DAY

1

Out on Long Island, the Beginning

I n 2003, Funny Cide became the first New York bred to win the Kentucky Derby. Although some said he'd had a lucky trip on the first Saturday in May, he followed with a masterful, dominating victory at the Preakness which silenced most doubters and created a buzz that swept the city and took up the front page of most newspapers. All the ink said maybe he was the real thing, our big horse, our Triple Crown winner. He wasn't, but the possibility changed the lives of his owners, his trainers, and me.

Here's how it happened: I had been writing book reviews and features for the fledgling *New York Sun*. The paper was a year old, and in April it added a sports page. I begged an assignment to go report on the biggest race of the year at Aqueduct, and really the only Kentucky Derby prep race that is run in New York, April's Wood Memorial. I'd been a fan of racing all my life, since I used to sit at the rail in Charles Town, West Virginia, with my parents and a picnic, since my grandfather took me to see the flamingos in the infield at beautiful old Hialeah in Florida. I'd never thought about being a sportswriter, but it seemed natural enough to write about a horse race.

That year's big horse was not Funny Cide. Stallions with rich bloodlines triumph in the classic three-year-old stakes races, and Funny Cide wasn't one of those. Funny Cide wasn't a stallion. He was a gelding (one of his testicles hadn't descended, and he'd been castrated as a result). A syndicate of upstate New Yorkers, all very obviously not the blue-blooded, private-jet type who are supposed to dominate the races, owned him. His trainer, Barclay Tagg, was not exactly the sort that typically stands in the winner's circle smiling after the million-dollar race. Tagg is the kind of smart, hardworking reserved trainer that horsemen love, but he doesn't typically win big stake races.

The big horse that year was Empire Maker. Coming onto the stretch in his last outing in the Florida Derby, he had blown by a horse named Trust N Luck, and had opened up nine and three-quarters lengths to win as if he were running in another league. And he looked the part: Empire Maker is a rippling, dappled, dark bay; the brown of his body fades to midnight at his feet and tail, and he stands just over sixteen hands, or sixty-four inches. At the Wood he was expected to further cement his position as the Derby favorite. Everyone knew it: Empire Maker was the horse.

I stood with my wife on the grass by the clubhouse turn for much of the day, and we watched a group of little children, three- and four-year-olds, run races against each other for hours. Their dads would take turns being the starting gates, finish lines, and pace cars, while the kids tirelessly toddled back and forth. Occasionally they would break out in a chant: "Empire Maker! Empire Maker! Empire Maker!" They were well-informed children.

It occurred to me then how straightforward this game is. Aside from all the hieroglyphic notations on the *Racing Form*, aside from all the traditions, the funny names, the personalities, and the money, it's a very simple game: run. First one there wins. Children understand it. Give them a name of who is going to win, and they understand that too.

The track was listed as muddy, but I remember sunshine. It was a pleasant day at the Big A. We were comfortable sitting in the grass on our jackets when our feet got tired. Nearby, a group of young New Yorkers, two couples, was having loud fun, teasing one another, falling asleep, and drinking beer in the sun.

A spring day at Aqueduct—this is as idyllic as New York City gets.

By the time the Wood came around, the crowd had bet the big Empire Maker down to be the overwhelming favorite at 1-2. The speed horse New York Hero had taken some action too, because of his name. Speed, in racing, doesn't mean exactly what one might think. Obviously the horse that runs the fastest will win the race, but that horse is not necessarily said to have speed. Speed means that the horse is a front-runner: he gets out of the gate fast and rushes to the lead. It's a very hard way to win races. The horse that leads early rarely has the strength to close the deal. Man o' War, among others, certainly proved that a horse vastly better will prevail no matter. New York Hero wasn't vastly better. He was not about to prevail, no matter what the crowd thought of his name. He was overmatched.

New York Hero would do what an overmatched speed horse must do: attempt to steal the race. He would jump to the front and try to set a false pace, leaving some gas in the tank for later. By the time he had nothing left, maybe all the other horses would have fallen into a sinkhole or all the jockeys would have fallen off. You never know.

When the gates clanged open, it was New York Hero out front, and people were cheering for him as he led the field through all the early segments of the race—the splits. Racing is typically divided into quarter-miles, which are further divided into furlongs, which are an eighth of a mile. Horses that are running perfectly run a furlong in about twelve seconds. Secretariat won the Belmont Stakes by thirty-one lengths because he ran perfect twelve-second furlongs all around the track. The splits are important elements in understanding how a race is unfolding. New York Hero ran the first quarter in 23.5 seconds, the half in 47.21, and six furlongs in 1:11.19. Averaging just under twelve seconds per furlong. This was no false pace. He was running as fast as he could. He'd never make it.

Sure enough, at the top of the stretch, New York Hero gave way. Empire Maker had been wide around all the turns, well within striking distance, rating just off the pace—letting New York Hero burn himself out—alongside Funny Cide.

Now Empire Maker gained the lead. In Florida this had been all she wrote. Empire Maker had made his move at the top of the stretch, and the field had melted away behind him, slogging along like pack mules.

But here at the Wood, Funny Cide came at him. Empire Maker opened it up. Funny Cide came at him again. I was astonished. They went under the wire like that. Funny Cide on the inside, running his heart out trying to get up past Empire Maker, while the big horse on the outside looked like he was playing. Empire Maker was watching the crowd when he went under the wire, ears perked. He was out for a jog. Empire Maker might as well have been playing golf.

That's what everyone picked up: Empire Maker toys with the competition to romp home in the $750,000 Wood Memorial. No argument from me on that. But what I'd seen was Funny Cide. He tried twice. That's saying something. That's guts.

By the time they hit the wire, Empire Maker and Funny Cide were seven and a half lengths ahead of the field. In Florida, Empire Maker had left every other horse that far up the track. Here, Empire Maker had a half a length lead. His jockey, Jerry Bailey, said the horse was goofy, and that if he'd hit him, Empire Maker would have pulled off to a greater victory. As it was, the Wood was one of the fastest of the Derby Preps. Empire Maker had won by half a length, but Funny Cide had shown something real. I saw it. That was one gutsy gelding.

And he was going to the Derby. I wrote my piece on the Wood and pitched another on Funny Cide headed for the Derby. I hung around Barclay Tagg's barn and watched the routine. I leaned on the rail in the morning with the clockers and the jockey agents, observing the morning workouts. I met the vet. Occasionally I petted Funny Cide. Mostly I was ignored by Tagg and his crew, and I tried to stay out of the way.

They're busy folks. One of the things that most amazed me was that the work didn't stop. You're sending one horse to the Kentucky Derby, but you've still got to worry about your filly down at the other end of the barn that's having trouble breathing.

Finally, on my last day at Belmont, Tagg walked up and said, "Okay. Whaddaya need?"

When Tagg found himself in the news a lot, he was frequently described as "taciturn." I don't think that's fair, but he's certainly not a showy guy, nor is he effusively convivial. He's a wiry, balding, hard worker with a serious demeanor. He's spent his life outside, around horses, and it shows.

How'd you like the Wood?

"He had more poise in that race than I'd seen in him yet," Tagg said. "He learns something every day."

Can he go the Derby distance? Tagg admitted it was a grueling race but said that Funny Cide was built for it.

"He's got a good hind end. He could push through a brick wall."

Tagg praised Robin Smullen, his girlfriend, assistant trainer, and Funny Cide's exercise rider. "He's a hard horse to control," said Tagg. "He's strong. She's great with him."

What kind of race would favor him? "I'd like to see a race just like the Wood." Tagg paused, watching a handler rub Funny Cide down outside barn six. "But I'd like to win it."

My piece went into the paper as a small feature box on the bottom of the sports page: "Local Horse Makes Good." I left that "I'd like to win it" dangling at the end of the piece, as if it were a prediction. I quoted Tagg on the horse's suitability for the Derby distance. I listed his victories and strengths. I wrote: "You rarely root for the home team at the track. . . . But at the 129th Kentucky Derby tomorrow, New Yorkers have a strong home team to root for."

The Derby was a perfect race for Funny Cide. While the other horses fought incredible traffic, Funny Cide was coolly tucked in, just off the lead, like a quarterback in the pocket all the way around. The horses out front tore through fractions; they had nothing left when it came to the stretch. Empire Maker came up on the outside, and jockey Jose Santos tapped Funny Cide and told him to go. Funny Cide really opened up. Trainer Bobby Frankel's two magnificent horses, Peace Rules, who had hung a much harder race and stuck valiantly for third, and Empire Maker, the horse who had toyed with Funny Cide so recently, couldn't get up to him on the first Saturday in May. Funny Cide broke into the lead on the stretch, and Tom Durkin's call of that race gave him a nickname he has to this day: "The Gutsy Gelding Funny Cide has won the 129th Kentucky Derby."

My little article in the *Sun* was now buried under a mountain of press about the local horse and the modest Sackatoga Stable. Suddenly, television cameras were at Tagg's barn. Everyone was coming by to congratulate them. The next time I saw Barclay Tagg and Robin Smullen, they barely remembered who I was.

But there it was, I'd scooped the Funny Cide story, albeit in a very small way. Still, I had him. Feels pretty good after a horse that breaks all the Derby rules (New York breds don't win the Derby, geldings don't win the Derby, Barclay Tagg doesn't win the Derby) slips under the wire.

It was also my first evidence of what it means to be a Sportswriter—a writer for a part of the paper that people read and argue about. I had talked briefly with the doorman of a building in which I worked in Manhattan about Funny Cide. My advice was no stronger than "Don't count him out." So the guy put him in all his trifecta bets. (A trifecta is a very hard bet to win. You have to name the win, place, and show horse in a race. Most of the time, you'll be wrong about any one of those slots.) This guy, like a lot of guys, bets a great deal of trifecta wagers on one race. You can do this—make fifty small wagers of a buck or two on a race—because the payoffs on a trifecta can be very big. He won something like six hundred dollars. For a while after the Derby, it was hard for me to get through the lobby and up to the office. Who do you like in the Preakness, Max?

Funny Cide.

The Triple Crown consists of three old races at three old tracks. It starts at the Kentucky Derby, then moves to Baltimore for the Preakness, and ends in New York for the Belmont Stakes. These are races for three-year-olds only. One of the tricks of the Triple Crown is that each of the races demands a different kind of horse. Barclay Tagg had told me that if it weren't for the owners, he wouldn't have even sent Funny Cide to Kentucky. Owners want their horse in the Kentucky Derby. That's why you own horses. Owning horses at all gets you into a pretty good club. Even a small stake in a syndicate will get you an owner's license that, if properly displayed, can get you whisked off to the Royal Enclosure at Ascot, and the air doesn't get much rarer than that, except perhaps when you're at Churchill Downs, and one of your horses is in the Derby.

But Tagg had told me that Funny Cide was a horse for the Preakness: "If I was smart I wouldn't even go to the Derby. He's a Preakness horse. He's going to love Pimlico."

And he did. Empire Maker was out with a bruised foot, resting up until the Belmont Stakes. Funny Cide crushed the short field and won it opening up daylight and looking like a champ.

So by the time we got to Belmont, the stakes were high. There were still those who believed that Funny Cide did not deserve to be placed among the few brilliant horses that had taken the Triple Crown. He was no Citation, they said, he was no War Admiral. Of course they were right, but he didn't have to be that good. All he had to do was win the Belmont Stakes.

The Belmont Stakes is the most difficult race in America. At a mile and a half, it is longer than any American three-year-old horse runs over dirt. The clubhouse turn at Belmont is very rarely used, because the track is so long that you can run most distances without rounding it. The sand is deep there. The turns are long, sweeping things. The backstretch is like the coast of Florida: endless sand. It's difficult for jockeys to run a mile and half, because their mental clocks—the little thing in their heads that knows that the pole they just flew by at forty miles per hour represented a quarter-mile left in the race, and now is the time to move—they've got to set that clock to daylight savings in order to time the Stakes properly.

To run a good race in the Belmont Stakes would be hard even if a horse were running it alone. But of course there's plenty of competition.

Still, it's only one race. It's only two and half minutes.

Belmont Park was bursting at the seams. 101,864 people were there to see Funny Cide take his shot. I was up in the third-deck grandstand seats. It's my favorite spot at Belmont, up in the cheap seats about halfway down the stretch. I've sat everywhere there is to sit at Belmont. I've sat in owner's boxes, I've sat at the restaurant, I've covered every inch of the rail. I've watched from the press box. I prefer the grandstand side of the rail, always, and the nosebleed grandstand seats. What you get up there is an incredible sense of the stretch run. It's very long (1,097 feet). You watch the horses come out of the turn, and they all make their run, and you watch them fight for it. Halfway down the stretch they reach where you're sitting. You turn your head and realize that while you thought they were almost there, they are only halfway done with the battle. It gives you a great sense of the what's special about Belmont: the size of the place.

Belmont typically feels big in the way an airport feels big when no one is traveling. Maybe there are some people hustling through the hush in the distance, but you could be alone somewhere if you wanted to be. Most of the year, Belmont is a good place for a quiet picnic.

But a big race day is different. People are everywhere. Beer is flowing. Hats are being sold. The betting lines are long. At Belmont, tickets to get into the biggest race of the year are still only two dollars. And the crowd is filled with people who may see one race a year. Or this might be the only race they'll ever see.

On that early June day in 2003, it began raining at 9:15 in the morning. By the time the stakes came around, everyone was soaked. The track was a mess.

But more than a hundred thousand people now look at their program and realized that the time has come. The next race on the card is the big one. The mood is charged. People find their spots. Everyone starts talking loudly.

In the grey, the mounted police take to the field, pretending they are giving some kind of a show and getting cheered as if they are. The brass band marches into the infield. A very drunk man sits down next to me, thanks me, and then gets up and leaves. The band plays "New York, New York."

You've been standing around all day, and now your feet no longer hurt. It's been raining all day, but you're no longer bothered by the wet.

At the paddock, where the horses are saddled and the jockeys go up before the race, a crush of fans is scrambling for a glimpse of the hero. Santos gets on him, and they walk to the track with an outrider pony for the post parade, where the horses calmly walk in front of the crowd, advertising their strengths and nodding their heads in that peculiar tick that thoroughbreds have. When Funny Cide hits the track, the crowd goes berserk.

One of the slickered outriders rears his horse. The big brown horse paws at the sky as if he were in an old Western; the crowd cheers and calls for more.

The horses have reached the starting gate.

"And they're off!"

The air seems to quiver, your senses expand, and you are sucked into the race. This, after all, is really it. In two and a half minutes either there will be a Triple Crown winner or there won't be. It's too real. Too vivid to be processed properly. You can't stop and think. You just soak up all the sensory input. I can only relate it to a wedding. You work for a long time, there's an awful lot of fanfare, everyone is dressed up and excited, and then something happens, it doesn't take long, but it marks a line in history. Two minutes ago you weren't married. Now you are. Moments ago Funny Cide was a local hero with a limitless future. Now, the gates have opened, and the horses have lunged onto a soaked track.

Going into the clubhouse turn, jockey Jerry Bailey takes Empire Maker to the outside, and Santos takes Funny Cide out to the lead.

Just like that, it was all over for Funny Cide, and Santos knew it. "He was switching leads back and forth, and I knew I was in big trouble. I didn't like him switching leads going into the first turn."

The crowd is still screaming. The hero has the lead. I sit down. How long had that been? Twenty-three seconds? The race was done.

When the half-mile fraction came up 48.7 seconds, I felt another glimmer. It's a respectable speed, "honest enough," as track announcer Tom Durkin called it, but not blazing. Perhaps Funny Cide would have the strength to run the race wire to wire.

But Jerry Bailey knew better. Up in the irons on the soon-to-be-victorious Empire Maker, he said he knew he'd won when they came out of the clubhouse turn. "Pulling up on the back stretch, I saw Funny Cide pulling on Jose." Horses want to run, and a jockey's job is to hold them back until the right moment. A horse that is too anxious won't settle into a pace but will literally yank at the reins. Bailey said: "My horse was very relaxed, and in a one-and-a-half-mile race, that's what you need."

Empire Maker tracks Funny Cide through the backstretch, stalking him like a big cat.

With a quarter-mile left to race, looking calm and strong, Bailey makes his move. A horse named Ten Most Wanted goes with him.

When they range up on Funny Cide, Santos asks for more. Funny Cide tries to give it to him. He doesn't have it.

Empire Maker watches Ten Most Wanted run along beside him, just as he had watched Funny Cide in the Wood. In the deep slop, Empire Maker is playing games.

Jerry Bailey, on his way to the winner's circle, where he would pluck carnations from the blanket draping Empire Maker and toss them to members of the horse's party, told his outrider, "He's a good horse, maybe a great horse. It's going to be a shame if they boo him." They booed, but Bailey understood. "I think it's disappointment about Funny Cide, not anger at Empire Maker."

The whole thing took 2:28.26. In wagers $12,973,555 had been laid down, and it took just over 148 seconds to figure out where it was going. Two and a half minutes ago, everyone was screaming and applauding an outrider, and the cops looked like they were on parade. Now it was a grim, rainy day, and there was a depressing hush over the crowd.

At a reading speed of two hundred words per minute, which is average, it took you longer to read about the race than it did to run it.

If you were to run all the Belmont Stakes that have ever been run back to back, all 136 of them, you'd be done in less than six hours. Fewer than six football games. Two baseball games. Three movies. A workday is two hours longer than the entirety of time spent on the track running the Belmont Stakes.

It's a very concentrated sport. Horse racing is like moonshine—it's the white lightning of sports, 190 proof. Horse racing is sport distilled.

This distillation of the sport, this concentrated, flat-out run over a short distance, is what America brought to the game. Races used to be longer. They used to consume all of a day. In America in the early nineteenth century, they got shorter. Just like the events that led to me being a turf writer, American racing began on Long Island.

Somewhere near Kennedy Airport, in what is now a mess of asphalt, car dealerships, boulevards, and two- to four-story apartment buildings, there was once a track named the Union Race Course. It was here that some unknown genius looked out over his sod and got tired of patching it up.

Outside of the desert, horses had run over grass for as long as horses had run. Across the world, the great majority of races are still run on grass. When Governor Nichols had what is generally considered to be the very first measured track in America paced off (also on Long Island) in the early seventeenth century, it was, like all the tracks before it, grass.

Think about what horses running top speed do to grass: they tear it up. You can't run too many races on a given patch of it, because it will soon be pocked with divots. The grass will be a mushy green pulp. So this fellow, whoever he was, decides, "Forget the grass, I'm going to skin the track." He peeled back the sod and raked a measured oval of dirt. He must have leaned against his rake with a feeling of nervous pride. Here was the track. Let them run on dirt. Will this work? With that simple act of American efficiency, laziness, and pragmatism, American racing was born.

Not only could you run more races on dirt, but the horses liked it. It seemed horses ran faster on dirt than on turf. It had taken years for folks to figure out that if they ran races in an oval they could see the whole race, but that had been the last basic advance in the sport. Dirt racing changed everything.

It was here, at America's first American-style track, that racing began its ascension. At the Union Race Course, what had been a sideline, a hobby of the rich and Anglophilic, became something else, something quintessentially American and exceedingly popular.

One of the early superstars of the sport was the brilliant horse American Eclipse. He was named after the most influential stallion of all time, the undefeated English horse Eclipse, foaled in 1764 like something out of mythology, during an eclipse of the sun.

American Eclipse was the foal of Duroc and Messenger. Duroc was a son of Diomed, the most important thoroughbred to reach American shores, the winner of the first Epsom Derby in England. Diomed wasn't a complete failure at stud in England, but he was no great shakes. Interest waned enough that at age twenty-one the stallion was sold for fifty guineas—not much. Within months, two Virginians, Colonel John Hoomes of Bowling Green, and John Tayloe III of Mount Airy, contacted their English agent, James Weatherby (the author of the first General Stud Book), to inquire about Diomed. Weatherby said to keep looking; the old horse was a "tried and proven bad foal-getter." Ignoring Weatherby's advice, Hoomes and Tayloe purchased the horse for a thousand guineas.

Even at that absurd inflation of price, Hoomes and Tayloe got the good end of the deal. They stood Diomed for half a season and sold him for six times what they'd paid. Diomed would live until he was thirty-one, and would stand stud at many farms before Hoomes bought him back late in life.

American Eclipse was Diomed's grandson, which makes him one of the early entries into the studbook that lists thousands of descendants of Diomed. All of them, on some morning out at the barn when they first stood up on spindly legs, were looking pretty promising.

Bred by General Nathaniel Coles, American Eclipse's morning came May 25, 1814. He was weaned on November 10 and, according to *Wallace's Monthly*, "gave his owner such an exhibition of his stride, strength and speed that he named him American Eclipse, believing he would render that name as illustrious on this side of the ocean." He had a pretty soft life, it seems, until he was first shod in March 1817. They trained him for a year. In late May 1818 he won his first race. The following year he was sold.

Moralizers are always pushing blue laws, and in 1820 racing was made illegal in New York, and American Eclipse was retired undefeated to spend the year at stud, for the low fee of $12.50. General Coles had sold Eclipse to Cornelius Van Ranst for three thousand dollars, and Van Ranst had been able to race him only twice. But the next year the legislation that had prohibited racing was repealed, and on October 15 Union Race Course was opened. The president of the Union Course, John Cox Stevens, asked Van Ranst to bring American Eclipse out of retirement for the feature that day. Eclipse met the Southern mare Lady Lightfoot, winner of thirty-one races. The purse was five hundred dollars, and the race would be run in four-mile heats. American Eclipse won in two heats. His greatest accomplishment still lay ahead.

In 1823, in Washington, D.C., Van Ranst met James Harrison of Virginia for a match race, Eclipse versus Sir Charles. Sir Charles had won twenty races. He was a formidable opponent, but he was not sound. He made it through three miles and broke down. The rest of racing was canceled.

But the rivalry was only invigorated. That evening at dinner, Colonel William R. Johnson was intent on continuing the challenge. John C. Stevens, president of Union Course, was there and proclaimed that American Eclipse would beat any horse the Southerners had the following spring. The purse in Washington had been five thousand dollars, and the enthusiastic horsemen bumped it up to twenty grand. The Southern faction was not required to name its entry until post time. Like the great English horse, his namesake, the Northerners believed, "Eclipse first, the rest nowhere."

In pictures of the Union Race Course, the place is invariably crowded. It was a two-level building, seemingly little more than a hotted-up hayloft in the middle of a field with American flags flying at either end. No doubt the champagne corks zipped through the air.

Here is a description of a similar North/South match race. Although it was held later than the twenty-thousand-dollar matchup, the details reported in the *Brooklyn Eagle* do more to set the stage than anything I've found:

"Just before the horses were to start, the crowd on the outside became impatient, tore down a length of fence and stove through a door in the stand and swarmed into the cleared place. For a short time the greatest excitement prevailed, and some of the more timid secured the services of Yankee Sullivan and other famous strongmen of the day to clear the course, which they did in very short time, by organizing a party of their friends, who formed into line with clasped hands and marched from one end back to the other, driving outside of the gates every person without a badge. In the crowd were many tough men, but the terrible right of Yankee Sullivan and gamey reputation of his followers made it very dangerous for anyone to contradict them."

Eventually Yankee Sullivan employed a bullwhip to bring order to the crowd. Meanwhile the people gambled at roulette, faro, three-card monte, and all manner of swindles and games.

In 1823 the scene couldn't have differed much. Contemporary accounts have it that the road to Union Course was completely clogged by 1:00 P.M., and that many of the reported sixty thousand spectators had arrived the night before. Twenty thousand were said to have come from the South. A system of signals was devised to relay the results of each heat to New York City as quickly as possible. If American Eclipse won a heat, a white flag would be flown. If the Southern horse edged him out, a black flag would be raised.

The Southerners produced another descendant of Diomed, the four-year-old Sir Henry. Eclipse was to be ridden by William Crafts. John Walden had the mount on Henry.

Cadwallader R. Colden's coverage of the race, which he observed mounted on a fast horse following the racers, is a famous piece of turf writing. (We still call it turf writing, regardless of the fact that there's no turf.)

"Henry, apparently the quickest, made play from the score, obtained the lead, and was then taken in hand. By the time they'd gone the first quarter of a mile . . . he was full three lengths ahead."

They tore around the dirt track. On the stretch, Crafts sent Eclipse up to challenge.

"Crafts was making every exertion with both spur and whip to get Eclipse forward, and scored him sorely both before and behind the girths. At this moment Eclipse threw his tail into the air, flirted it up and down, after the manner of a tired horse, or one in distress or great pain. . . . The rider of Henry turned his head around to take a view of his adversary. Walden used neither whip nor spur . . . Crafts continued to make free use of the whip; his right hand, in so doing, was necessarily disengaged from the bridle, his arm often raised high in the air, his body thrown abroad, and his seat loose and unsteady. . . . He had thrown himself quick back to the cantle of the saddle, stuck his feet forward by way of bracing himself with the aid of the stirrups . . . rocking to and fro, belaboring the horse, from right to left, girth to flank."

Henry won the heat in record time. Up went the black flag. Word spread. The stock market plummeted.

Eclipse was in sorry shape, bleeding profusely from the cuts lashed into him by Crafts. I can't imagine that anyone, especially Eclipse, was very fond of Crafts about now.

Samuel Purdy, a retired jockey gone slightly grey, had come to the track with his gear on under his overcoat. Some evidence disputes this, but there is no doubt that Purdy, who had ridden Eclipse in the past, stepped forward and was given the mount.

He brought the game to Henry. Josiah Quincy, who was seated behind the noted Virginian John Randolph, recorded in his diary that "Sir Henry took the inside track and held it for more than two miles and a half. Eclipse followed close on his heels and tried to pass. At every spurt he made Randolph's high-pitched and frustrating voice was heard. Each time shriller than before, 'You can't do it, Mr. Purdy! You can't do it, Mr. Purdy! You can't do it, Mr. Purdy!' But Mr. Purdy did do it, and as he took the lead what a roar of excitement went up." Quincy wrote that while he had nothing riding on the race, he lost his breath with the excitement "and felt as if a sword passed through [him]."

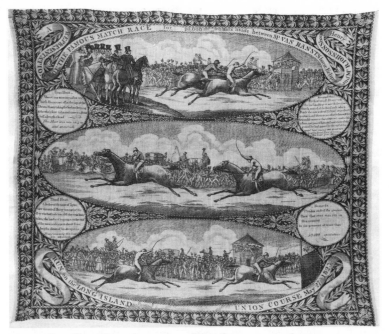

Print of a silk telling the story of the famous race between Eclipse and Sir Henry at the Union Race Course, 1823.

Purdy steered Eclipse to the inside and, riding hard, pushed him clear of Henry by two lengths.

For the final heat, another jockey substitution was made. The trainer and retired jockey Arthur Taylor would ride Sir Henry.

In the Museum of the City of New York, I found a sheet of newspaper. Above the fold was an excellent reproduction of a chintz souvenir from the Union Race Course, documenting the race between Henry and Eclipse. Below the fold was an account by W. H. B. Cooper of the third heat: "Despite the wonderful recovery of the Northern horse, the Southerners still

[23]

continued to back their horse to the limit. . . . Purdy, by quick dash, got the lead, and pushing Eclipse with whip and spur maintained the advantage until about sixty rods from the finish. Here, Sir Henry, making a supreme effort, ran up to Eclipse and for a moment seemed to be passing him, but he could not keep the pace, and Eclipse won by three lengths in 8 minutes and 24 seconds." As the old print reproduced here says, "Thus ended the greatest race that was ever run in this country."

The white flag flew for the second time that day.

Colden, the old turfman on the horse, wrote that the roar "seemed to roll along the track, as the horses advanced, resembling the loud and reiterated shout of contending armies."

It would be forty years before that bit of metaphor would seem eerily portentous. Dirt-track racing, however, had arrived.

There are stories that a few Southerners had literally bet the farm that day, and having lost their plantations, committed suicide on the spot.

It seems almost to go without saying that American Eclipse was retired, this time for good, following the match race of May 27. He stood stud in New York, Kentucky, and Virginia before dying in Shelby County, Kentucky, at thirty-three.

2
That's Horse Racing

We've been racing horses since that first brave idiot sat on one back in the Stone Age. We've been racing as an organized, recorded sport for many hundreds of years. It is a sport drenched in tradition and clogged with ritual. Any sport so ritualized and ancient is bound to develop a library of clichés upon which the players rely. Some of the clichés are useful metaphors, others are sporting terms, and others are simply shorthand descriptions.

We've all decided that we know what we mean when we say, "That horse has a real turn of foot." We mean that the horse runs his race late, in the final furlongs on the stretch.

It is telling that I couldn't even describe one racing cliché without invoking another. When we say "runs his race" we mean that all but the very best thoroughbreds can make only one attempt at winning in any one race. When you stop holding them back and ask them to run, they run with all they've got, and they either get caught or not. That's why everyone takes notice when a horse manages to try again, and why we're all impressed with a horse that can flash some speed, then settle down, and then run again. Only the best horses can do these things. Most of them simply run their race.

The most prevalent phrase around the track is so ubiquitous that 999 times out of a grand it can go unsaid. You can communicate this cliché simply by arching your eyebrows, or smiling. It has always stood out to me.

"That's horse racing."

Which means that anything can happen. It is the prevailing spirit of the sport. Everybody says it over and over again, one way or another. I heard Jerry Bailey say it right around the time he was set to receive the plaque for winningest jockey of all time at Saratoga. They named a race after him that day, and it was the only race on the card in which he didn't have a mount. He was a late jockey substitution, and that's as good a reason as I've ever heard to put money on a horse's nose. What are they going to do? They're going to substitute him in to ride some plater (a weak-footed, slow horse) at the last second in the race that is named after him? I bet with both hands, and sure enough he was in the winner's circle to receive the plaque from the former winningest jockey, Angel Cordero, Jr. Anyway, it was right around this time, in reference to some race in which Bailey was in the irons on an overwhelming favorite, that he said, "You still have to go around the track before they give you the money."

Because anything can happen in horse racing. Some horses get lucky. Even Zippy Chippy—as of this writing a maiden at thirteen and the losingest thoroughbred in American history, having just notched his one hundredth loss at a fairgrounds in Northhampton, Massachusetts—could wake up one day and find that he really liked his oats and had the wind at his back. Just as every horse has his day, every horse can fail. A horse that's a dead certainty to romp home a whole furlong ahead of the field might stand in the gate looking as if he's never set foot on a racetrack.

Many folks out in the barns, on what's called the backside, will not tell you how they think their horse will do. I saw Shug McGaughey coming out of his barn at Belmont Park one day, the morning of the Acorn Stakes. He had a pretty good horse in the race, named La Reina. We said good morning to each other, not because he recognized me but because I said it first, and then I said, "You got something in the Acorn this afternoon, don't you?" He nodded. "La Reina?" I asked. He corrected my pronunciation. "Whaddaya think? How's she gonnna do?" He looked at the dirt path he was walking on and zipped up quick. I don't even think he shook his head in disgust. All I wanted was a little race talk and an opportunity to wish him luck, but I'd stepped on his toes by suggesting that anyone, anywhere, has any real idea how a race will be run.

That's horse racing.

It's proven every day at tracks all over the country. But Saratoga—sometimes called the Graveyard of Favorites—has a special place in the history of crazy luck. Man o' War lost only one race in his career, and he did it on August 13, 1920, as a two-year-old, to a horse named Upset in the Sanford Stakes at Saratoga. Supposedly—at least this is what horse people say—we didn't use the word "upset" to describe the defeat of a favorite before Upset's upset. Secretariat lost a few races over his twenty-one starts (Man o' War and Secretariat both raced twenty-one times), but the most surprising loss came at Saratoga, after he had won the Triple Crown. Secretariat had just romped in Chicago at an Arlington Park invitational and had brought his margin of victory over just the last two races to *forty* lengths. Forty lengths leaves the opposition very far up the track. Secretariat was invincible, he set world records, he was a superstar. Five thousand people showed up to watch him work out over a half-mile at Saratoga before his next scheduled race, the Whitney, in which there was an Allen Jerkins colt rather humbly named Onion. Secretariat versus a horse named Onion? Give me a break. But Secretariat was working badly, and Onion was ready. They ran at each other on the stretch. Onion pulled away and came under the wire a length ahead.

That's horse racing.

The truth is that chalk (meaning favorites) wins at Saratoga as much as it does everywhere—but there's something in the air. You don't want to be the overwhelming favorite if you're a champion. If the whole world thinks you can't lose, look out. Just think about the English. After all, the first upset at Saratoga wasn't a horse race: it was war.

In 1777, British general John Burgoyne was marching south from Canada with the idea that he'd split the colonies in two. The old "Divide and Conquer." On July 6, Burgoyne took Fort Ticonderoga in New York, and by July 29 his army had reached the upper Hudson River. In September the army marched in three columns (one of them made up of German troops) through the land that would now comprise the towns of Saratoga Springs and Stillwater. The Germans were marching along the river, and the two columns of British troops were marching through the tall pines of the forest. Colonel Daniel Morgan's Virginia Riflemen tracked them, and they engaged at a place called Freeman's Farm. Burgoyne held the field but was left in poor shape after three hours of heavy fighting. The royals entrenched and waited for support from the south, which never came.

On October 7, his army weary, hungry, and weakened, no doubt sensing that winter would hit soon enough, Burgoyne decided to move. His army set out, and the Americans attacked. The second battle of Saratoga was on.

It was a fine day for Benedict Arnold. He led a series of attacks on the Balcarres Redoubt at Freeman's Farm, but failed to take it. He rode instead to another of the British field fortifications called the Breymann Redoubt. The Americans overwhelmed the German troops defending the position, and took the fortification. Arnold was wounded entering the redoubt. If he'd quit that day and drifted off to retirement in Kentucky or someplace pleasant, he'd be remembered as a hero.

The Brits retreated and encamped on the Saratoga Heights, where they were surrounded by twenty thousand American troops. On October 17, Burgoyne surrendered.

The French decided that this victory was proof enough and commenced open support of the American cause. They had been sneaking us money and help all along, but this spurred them on. Benjamin Franklin wrote to George Washington from France that another defeat like Saratoga would sway public opinion in favor of the Colonists. It would be years until victory at Yorktown, but Saratoga was an important step.

Although the father of the nation wasn't there, he soon visited Saratoga. Waiting for the Paris treaty to be signed, George Washington was doing a bit of touring, and on his list of must-sees was the site of the battle of Saratoga. He was traveling with Francesco dal Verme, an Italian count, and the governor of New York, George Clinton. The day they visited the springs at Saratoga, they were drunk. Apparently it was a local custom to drink spirits as an antidote to the fog (anti-fogmatics), and the fog was thick that day. The group drank their lunch and wandered out into the Saratoga fog on horseback to look at the mineral springs.

Indians had used the waters medicinally; they were said to have great curative effects. Washington was impressed. He soon wrote to the governor and asked about purchasing Saratoga Springs. That the Colonists had won such an important battle at the site put the name Saratoga high in people's minds, with excellent connotations. Washington seems to have been sure that the quality of the springs, the beauty of the place, and the name recognition guaranteed that this could be a very successful resort town. He had seen how prosperous these watering places could be in the spring towns of Virginia, such as Bath. For more than a year he tried to buy Saratoga Springs, but the locals wanted the place for themselves. Edward Hotaling points out in his excellent book *They're Off!* that in this way the locals set up a kind of a tradition of tourists being "foiled by the natives" and undoubtedly did the nation a great service. No one, not even Washington, wants to leave Saratoga to go to his job.

Washington was right about Saratoga Springs. It soon became America's premier resort, advertised by the widely available Congress Water that was bottled and shipped in quantities so large that moratoriums eventually were placed upon taking the water so that the spring could replenish itself.

In 1825, Horatio Gates Spafforg published *The Gazetteer of the State of New York, Embracing an Ample Survey of Its Counties, Towns, and Villages, Canals, Mountains, Lakes, Rivers, Creeks, and Natural Topography.* Of Saratoga Springs he wrote: "The Village is handsomely laid out, and besides many taverns and hotels, private dwellings and boarding houses, of common form and size, has three Hotels, of enormous dimensions, for Summer Visitants. The Congress Hall, Pavilion, and Union Hall merit enumeration, at least. In the season of company, which continues but about three months, and hardly so long, for the butterflies of fashion, all these houses are full to overflowing, and yet every family takes boarders. The Village has a Printing Office, a Reading Room, and Circulating Library, and all sorts of amusements for all sorts of people. No place in America has a greater resort of company, and none in the world a richer variety of Mineral Waters."

Of the county, Spafforg wrote: "The agriculture of this County is very respectable, and yet there is much room for improvement. It has a spirited Agricultural Society, which seems to be doing much good. It receives 300 dollars a year from the State. The towns are minutely described, and I am weary of my task. Bog iron ore is found in Milton and Saratoga Springs, and some in a few other towns, and some mountain, magenetic iron ore, in the NW towns. . . . The Mineral Waters of this County are of high celebrity. It may be safely computed that the resort of company to these Watering

Places, is annually worth 60,000 to 100,000 dollars, about the sum usually left in this county, every year, by Visitants. Did they not leave their habits, their pride, their extravagance, and follies, this great sum would be very beneficial to the inhabitants."

The Visitants might leave their money, their pride, and their follies behind in Saratoga, but it was not yet due to horse racing. The first race in Saratoga would not be run until 1847. It was a trotting race, with wagons, and the winner was the old grey mare herself (the one from the song, "She ain't what she used to be"), Lady Suffolk. It was run as a part of a fair—an exhibition of speed—and attracted a grand crowd, including two former presidents (John Tyler and Martin Van Buren), one future president (Millard Fillmore), and General Tom Thumb. Saratoga was on its way, and the character who would truly deliver it was just then trudging around New York City looking for something to do.

Pugilist, gambler, and politician, John Morrissey brought racing to Saratoga. His name is attached to no document in connection with the development of the track, but his involvement was not well concealed. In 1869 there were no buildings in Saratoga attributed to the (much more respectable) men with whom Morrissey worked. Morrissey, however, is all over the town, including connections to the Saratoga Pool Room, a clubhouse, and two cottages moved from the Grand Union Grounds.

Bellicose only begins to describe John Morrissey. He had been born in Tipperary in 1831. At five, his folks took him to Quebec, and then they drifted south to Troy, New York.

John Morrissey: pugilist, gambler, politician—and the man who brought racing to Saratoga.

Young John gathered some small education before working in a paper mill, an ironworks, as a bartender for a noted "sportsman" named Alexander Hamilton, and as a bouncer in a whorehouse, all the while gaining note as a pugilist and a street fighter. He was deeply involved in the feuds between the young street toughs of Troy and West Troy. He worked in an iron shop in Troy alongside a young man named John C. Heenan during the day, and at night they fought on opposite sides in what the *Brooklyn Eagle* referred to as "many a sanguinary affray." Morrissey worked as a deckhand on the steamboat *City of Troy*, whose captain was his future father-in-law Levi Smith. It was during their trips up and down the river that Morrissey took up with Smith's daughter Susie.

Morrissey found his fortune and success in the professional boxing ring. He defeated George Thompson on August 31, 1852, to win the championship of California and two thousand dollars. He also won five thousand dollars at the races in Santa Barbara.

In 1853 he returned to New York. On October 12, Morrissey fought thirty-seven rounds with Yankee Sullivan. Both men were stomped, but only Morrissey could get up and enter the ring to continue, so he was declared the victor of the vicious battle. He would fight only once more, this time against his old co-worker and fellow street tough John Heenan. Heenan had become a very serious boxer, and the fight between the two was to be for the championship of America. On October 20, 1858, they beat the hell out of each other. Morrissey was covered in blood, but after eleven rounds he was standing and Heenan was out.

Morrissey had advised Fernando Wood in his quest for the mayorship of New York City in 1854, and Wood had won it. Morrissey had met and befriended President Lincoln. Morrissey's gambling houses in New York had turned him into America's most famous gambler and given him substantial wealth.

Meanwhile, life in Saratoga became grander and grander. It was neck and neck with Newport as a splendid vacation spot. The chef at Moon's Lake House (a very swank joint) had learned to slice potatoes very thin and fry them, thereby inventing the Saratoga Chip, which we now know as the potato chip. The hotels were the biggest anyone could think of. Edward Hoagland wrote that "In 1860, Appleton's Hand-book suggested 'Saratoga . . . probably always will be the most famous place of summer resort in the United States.'"

JUST AS WAR played a part in the birth of Saratoga, so war influenced the beginning of racing there. When the lead began flying around Fort Sumter, America went to war with itself, and all of the great meets of Southern thoroughbred racing were ended. Some tried to persist, but by December 1861 all were closed. Kentucky was a neutral state with a lot of horseflesh, and its horsemen soon sent their animals north to a quickly developed racing circuit. Thoroughbred racing had not been popular in the North; in 1861 only one meet was held in the Northeast. But by 1863 there was a circuit. And Morrissey was on it.

His first meet at Saratoga was run over Horse Haven, which now encircles some stables. You can still walk the track. It's weedy and narrow, the turns tight beside little outbuildings, and it abuts a parking lot on the backside, but it's worth it. The security guard standing at Union Avenue will know why you're doing it, and he'll love the idea. This is, after all, Saratoga.

Fifteen thousand people attended that first meet. There were wonderful upsets and excellent rumors, and the bars on Broadway buzzed with race talk. The Saratoga hotels were jammed, filled to capacity and turning people away.

The day after the races ended, Commodore Cornelius Vanderbilt raised ten thousand in two hours, three thousand of it his own, to begin the formation of the Saratoga Association. William Travers was named president. Leonard Jerome and John Purdy (son of Sam Purdy, the jockey of American Eclipse) were vice presidents. They bought ninety-four acres across the street from Horse Haven.

Morrissey, though it was his energy and his importation of talent that had started the whole thing, was removed from prominence. He was given an executive position, but the organizers of the Saratoga Association did not wish the public to think that America's first modern sports business was funded and run by a crazy gambling street fighter.

By the next year, 1864, Saratoga as we know it, more or less, was there. The racetrack building has changed some, but from comparing old pictures of the place to my own pictures, I'd say not much.

There is nothing like it. There is no air conditioning, and on warm days ceiling fans whir above the wooden stands. Aside from the kitchens and the press box, I don't think there's even an enclosed room. The box seats are small, and in each you find light, bentwood chairs. Awnings are everywhere, red and white striped.

The seats are always filled. The aprons, that area by the rail where folks mill about and cheer on the horses, are always crowded. The smell of fried potatoes still wafts through the air on the fresh Adirondack breezes. It's hot in August, but not compared to New York City, and by the time one leaves Saratoga it has already begun to feel like autumn. At the gate a Dixieland band blows out a tune, serenading the iron lawn jockeys painted in the colors of the silks of last year's stakes winners. Inside, small jazz ensembles play. But that's not the sound you hear the most. What you do hear is endless horse talk. Everyone talks horses during the month-long meet. There's a sulfuric spring that's been renamed Big Red, in honor of Man o' War, and there's frothy beer and a betting window at every turn.

Two famous lines are said about Saratoga. The first is Joe Palmer's quip that "A man who would change it would stir champagne." The second is Red Smith's, who wrote: "To get to Saratoga Springs, you have to go about 175 miles north, turn left on Union Avenue, and go back 100 years."

I'm a fan of both of these sayings. Each of them makes me smile. But they don't point to what's fantastic about Saratoga. They are essentially nostalgic sentiments, after all, and what Saratoga has is not nostalgia. It's not about what's come before but rather about the vitality of the tradition. Racing in Saratoga is center stage. For six weeks the little town in upstate New York will see its population triple, until it is bursting at the seams with horsemen and punters.

At the Spa, as Saratoga is called, horse racing is on everyone's mind, the starting gate is always full, and the *Daily Racing Form* is the paper of record. And always, always, people are complaining. It's the graveyard of champions, after all, and what's supposed to happen often doesn't.

Never was that proved more conclusively than in the summer of 1930. Surely by then Saratoga must have lost some of its fin-de-siècle grandeur, or at least a bit of its hauteur. I'm sure the champagne had been shaken, stirred, emptied, refilled, and resold. The sixty-first Travers Stakes would go off on August 16, a scant ten months after Wall Street's dizzying crash. But the depths of the Great Depression were not what kept challengers away from the Midsummer Derby that year. They were scared off by a horse named Gallant Fox.

William Woodward, Sr., president at the time of racing's governing body, the Jockey Club, owned the Fox. Woodward had graduated from Harvard Law in 1903. He had worked in England for a time and there had learned to love racing, maintaining a stable at Newmarket. After his uncle handed over the presidency of the Hanover National Bank in 1910, Woodward inherited the Belair Stud in Maryland, which had operated as a horse farm for more than two hundred years. Woodward had three thousand manicured acres and a mammoth Georgian mansion—all red brick and boxwoods, with four chimneys jutting out of the main building—at the end of a long avenue of tall old oaks. Belair Stud itself was beautiful as well, a squat stone building with a generous arched center carriageway and cobblestone pavers.

Woodward had managed to cash out and somehow maintain his fortune when the stock market tumbled, and he still had what now must have appeared to be limitless wealth.

At Belair, Gallant Fox cavorted about the grounds as a yearling. He was the son of Sir Gallahad, a stallion imported by a syndicate headed up by A. B. Hancock, Sr., of Claiborne Farm in Kentucky. The Hancocks are historically adept at syndicates—decades later they syndicated Secretariat for record money. Sir Gallahad set the precedent, and Woodward was a member of the syndicate. In 1927, his first year at stud, they bred Sir Gallahad to Marguerite, and on March 23 she foaled a big bay colt, Gallant Fox.

Gallant Fox stayed at Claiborne Farm until he was a weanling, and was then shipped to Belair Stud. At two he was placed in the barn of Sunny Jim Fitzsimmons, one of history's best trainers.

When they built the old Sheepshead Bay racetrack in New York, they had to tear down the house in which Fitzsimmons was born to do it, but he wasn't away from that piece of ground for long. Fitz's first job was in the track kitchen there, in 1884, at the age of ten. By fifteen he was a jockey. A horse named Bartender gave him his first stakes victory in 1890. Within ten years he had left the irons and dedicated himself to training. Sunny Jim went to work for Woodward in 1923, and the match was magic.

Magic might not have been the word for the two-year-old Gallant Fox, however. At the 1929 Tremont Stakes at Aqueduct, Gallant Fox's second start, he was left in the gate due to his overpowering interest in a low-flying plane. He did not finish in the money at all that day. In the Futurity that same year, run at Belmont Park, he took the lead and slowed to a mild canter. Harry P. Whitney's colt Whichone ranged up on him and blew by to get under the wire. Gallant Fox barely hung on to show.

At the end of his two-year-old career, the Fox was a good horse—seven starts, two wins, two places, two shows—but hardly a champion, and certainly not indicative of what was to come. Woodward and Fitzsimmons seemed to know, though. His entire two-year-old career was really just a prep for the following year. He wintered at Belair, and by the spring he stood over sixteen hands high and weighed more than twelve hundred pounds. He was ready. All he needed was a jockey worthy of him.

Enter Earle Sande. Sande had begun his career as a local fairgrounds rider out West. By 1917 he was up on thoroughbreds in New Orleans. He was the leading rider of 1921, 1923, and 1927; he had ridden Zev to 10 stakes victories, had ridden Sir Barton, the first horse to sweep the Triple Crown, and had ridden Man o' War. Over the course of his life he rode 3,663 races and won 26 percent of them. Sande had been flirting with retirement as early as 1924 when he took a spill at Saratoga. In 1925 he won the Kentucky Derby on Flying Ebony. By 1930, however, he was training horses. To ride Gallant Fox, Woodward offered him 10 percent of the purse money instead of a retainer, his usual deal, and Sande came out of retirement.

The first race was the Wood Memorial, which was run at a mile and seventy yards at New York's Jamaica racetrack. Gallant Fox ran just off the pace and cruised to victory by four lengths.

He was the favorite in the Preakness, which in 1930 was run before the Derby. That year was the first time an electric starting gate was used in a classic race—it caused some controversy but didn't faze Gallant Fox. He won the thirty-ninth Preakness going away.

In the Derby, Gallant Fox was again the favorite, and again he won the race easily. It was Sande's third Derby victory, tying the record of the great jockey Isaac Murphy.

It had been wet at the Derby, but it was even wetter at Belmont. They were back at the scene of the Futurity, and

Whichone was going to the gate this time too. Gallant Fox ran that race wire to wire, repelling a late challenge from Whichone and opening three lengths to become the second winner of what was not yet called the Triple Crown.

Whichone and Gallant Fox naturally drew all the money at the Travers that August. There were two other horses in the race. Sun Falcon was a long shot at 30-1. Then there was Jim Dandy. No one, but no one, was looking at this Kentucky-bred horse from California that had spent the winter in Tijuana running at Aqua Caliente. His total earnings for the year were a meager $125. Of his twenty career starts he'd been out of the money in all but four. He was set to go off at 100-1. The heavy plunger Subway Sam Rosoff got even better odds than that. By one account, Max "Kid Rags" Kalik gave him 500-1 on the colt, and Sam took it for $500. By another, he bet a thousand. Either way, he was down on the longest shot on the board, and standing to make a bucketful if the impossible happened.

Jim Dandy had raced all over the place. He was running in Kentucky when James McKee was there to enter Naishapur in the Kentucky Derby. Naishapur took second, but what seemed to grab the trainer was a young colt who had just scored an upset in Spring Trial. He wasn't supposed to have a chance, but he won the race over an off track to pay forty-two dollars. McKee talked Chaffee Earl into coughing up twenty thousand for the two-year-old. At Saratoga he won the Grand Union Hotel Stakes against some tough competition and paid one hundred dollars. But these victories for Jim Dandy were few, and the initial investment must have looked at times pretty foolish.

McKee still had faith in the colt. He made it clear that his plan was to win the Travers. Although against Gallant Fox and Whichone, who could believe him?

Jim Dandy was working out at Tanforan, a track near San Francisco, and when it came time to ship east, he traveled in style. Naishapur and Jim Dandy occupied a coach designed for twelve horses, and their coach was hooked to the California Limited. The Santa Fe Railroad charged eighteen hundred dollars for the trouble.

How must McKee have felt when the *New York Times* reported that "Seldom has there been a race which so patently lay between two horses"?

The Travers was the fifth race on the card of six races for the day. August in Saratoga is a rainy time, and this was no exception. Post time was 5:20 P.M., and despite the clouds rolling in, some thirty thousand people had gathered to watch the Fox go up against Whichone. It had rained heavily all Friday and through the night. The track was rated as good.

As the horses were called to the post, it rained again. Gallant Fox had won the Belmont on a wet track; surely a little rain wouldn't bother him.

Jockey Red Baker had trained over with Jim Dandy, and although he had won only 5 percent of his starts, he was up in the irons, a late substitution for the much more successful Johnny Maiben. Jim Dandy would start from the second hole, to the outside of Sun Falcon, whose jockey was intently concerned about staying in the race for the show money, imagining like everyone else that the exacta was a sure thing. Whichone was in the three slot, and the Fox would pop out of the gate on the fourth path.

The start was good for all. Jim Dandy got a nose in front, but Sunny Workman, up on Whichone, hustled his mount to the lead. Sande and Gallant Fox settled in just alongside and they headed into the clubhouse turn just as they should be. Whichone was saving ground on the inside and clearly trying to establish an early advantage and tire the Fox, but Sande was confident, settling in and keeping the heat on Whichone. Sande rode like he had a lot of horse under him. Workman would ask Whichone for a little more, and Gallant Fox would stick right to him.

They dueled through the first quarter in an underwhelming twenty-five seconds.

Jim Dandy was tucked in on the rail running comfortably three and a half lengths off the lead. Sun Falcon trailed.

On the backstretch, Gallant Fox turned up the heat. The two leaders ran shoulder to shoulder. The Belair Fox put his head out front, and Whichone came right back at him. They picked up the pace; at three-quarters of a mile they clocked 1.13 3/5. They were still throwing mud at Jim Dandy at the top of the stretch turn. The race was on. The crowd was hollering. On the turn, Whichone found another gear and headed Gallant Fox, but the Fox responded yet again, roaring along on the outside and pulling even. Sonny Workman tried to shake him with some race riding. He drifted out off the rail, pushing Gallant Fox and Sande into the middle of the muddy track.

Sande could be a tough customer. Workman probably expected to be yanked out of the saddle for forcing him out like that.

Jim Dandy was now within a length. Red Baker had been holding him hard, pulling him back, but now he saw his hole and he let him go. Workman and Sande were so involved in their battle that neither seemed to notice Jim Dandy.

Thirty thousand people were startled into silence as Jim Dandy dashed by the two favorites. He was running on the rail, a chestnut blur, and by the time they clocked a mile in 1.42, the lead was all Jim Dandy. He was opening up daylight on the big horses.

At the top of the stretch, Whichone sagged and Gallant Fox finally shook him. Sande tried furiously to catch Jim Dandy, but Jim Dandy was going away. Five lengths. Jim Dandy was just galloping over the mud. Sande had his whip on the Fox, trying to coax one last charge out from him; the crowd was screaming for Gallant Fox to catch up. But Jim Dandy would not be caught. He was eight lengths in front of the Fox by the time he hit the wire. The first horse race ever to be broadcast on the radio had been a shocker. Subway Sammy Rosoff was screaming, "I got it! I got it! I got it!" He was suddenly $250,000 richer.

It was the only race Gallant Fox lost as a three-year-old. He retired at the end of the season, and back at Claiborne he sired Omaha, who went on to win the Triple Crown just like his daddy. Whichone popped a knee and bowed a tendon. Sonny Workman had to pull him up and walk him back to the scales; the horse never raced again.

Jim Dandy winning the Travers Stakes at Saratoga in 1930.

Jim Dandy stayed on the track until he was 12, eventually starting 141 times, of which he won only 7.

How could Jim Dandy have opened up like that in front of two first-class horses? Sonny Workman was asked that question in the flurry that followed the stunning upset.

He shrugged and said, "They just couldn't catch him."

Yep. That's horse racing.

3

Death in Memphis and a Fight on the Stretch

The Kentucky Derby has generated more passion, more ink, and more hyperbole than almost anything I can think of outside of sex and war. For two minutes in the spring, millions of dollars, dozens of dreams, and the maintenance of a national mythology are on the line.

Pretty much every horse in the race, all of them three years old, has been pointed to the Derby since the day it first stood on spindly legs and suckled. It's very rare that a horse gets to the Derby by accident. The horses that arrive in Louisville are the products of incredible genetic manipulation, as were their parents, and grandparents, and farther back. Their bloodlines have been carefully orchestrated to make the next big thing, the next splash, the next superstar on the track, and then in the breeding shed, where the real money is made. A horse that's won the Derby is worth a lot more as a stallion, and in thoroughbred breeding that's a lot of money. Glenye Caine, in her book about thoroughbred breeding, *The Home Run Horse,* writes of Taylor Made farm in Nicholasville, Kentucky: "The Farm now stands six stallions . . . their fees range from $10,000 for champions Artax and Real Quiet to $125,000 for Breeders' Cup Juvenile winner Unbridled's Song. Together, the Taylor Made stallions sired 409 foals in 2003 for North American breeders. If they sired the same number again in 2004, and if all those breeders were to pay the full stud fees, Taylor Made's stallion barn alone would generate $18,575,000."

But money doesn't explain the whole of it. Owners have lulled themselves to sleep thinking of the horse that would put them in the winner's circle, watching the governor of Kentucky raise a champagne toast in their direction.

For horsemen, the Derby represents three years of racing, feeding, grooming, and dreaming distilled down to two minutes. Some of these horses will have run as few as four or five times in their career; rarely will their experience exceed a dozen trips to the gate. If the horse ran a big race back on his first or second shot, and proved worthy of the blood in his veins and the money that hit the barrelhead at auction, he's been pointed to this day ever since. The trip to the Derby is like trying to land a horse on the moon. Everything must align properly. The margin for error is slim. The horse—a half-ton, high-strung, tightly wound, temperamental beast with zero communication skills and a proclivity for injuring himself—is both an astronaut and the rocket.

It's clear that trainers, owners, and jockeys have a lot invested in the Derby. All horsemen involved in the race are directly affected by its outcome. But, after all, that adds up to maybe one or two thousand people.

What about the rest of us?

Each year the Derby is the most-watched horse race on television. Each year Churchill Downs is flooded with revelers. Each year millions of dollars are pushed through the betting windows by people who wouldn't dream of laying down a place bet at Aqueduct in February.

William Faulkner wrote about the Derby for *Sports Illustrated* in 1955. His piece was madness. His opening line: "This saw Boone: the bluegrass, the virgin land rolling westward wave by dense wave from the Allegheny gaps, unmarked then, teeming with deer and buffalo about the salt licks and the limestone springs whose water in time would make the fine bourbon whiskey; and the wild men too—the red men and the white ones too who had to be a little wild also to endure and survive and so mark the wilderness with the proofs of their tough survival—Boonesborough, Owenstown, Harrod's and Harbuck's Stations; Kentucky: the dark and bloody ground." You don't get much of a sense of the race. But that anyone would even consider a pile of purple modernism like this as legitimate coverage of a sporting event tells you something about the Derby.

The following year—it must have been a bit of a fad in the 1950s to persuade literary lions to write about the Derby—John Steinbeck went to work for the *Louisville Courier-Journal.* Here's his lead: "At this sacred moment, in this place of pilgrimage, I have several towering but gossamer convictions. During Derby Week, Louisville is the capital of the world. This lively, lovely city has a temporary population of foster-citizens second only to China. I am also sure that if the national elections took place today, our next president would be a horse." Sacred moment, place of pilgrimage—again, we're up there in the stratosphere of the American imagination.

In June 1970, Hunter S. Thompson wrote a crazy and heavily amplified bender of misanthropic self-promotion for *Scanlans Monthly* in "The Kentucky Derby Is Decadent and Depraved." Again we get little racing, but Thompson's wild ride through Churchill Downs is entertaining and depraved. He imagines that the rotten, bloated, liquor-drunk hedonist who has murdered his vision of the American Dream must have a box seat around here somewhere.

I can think of little but the Kentucky Derby capable of supporting such attention. Most subjects would crack and shatter under the weight of the interest.

Shelves and shelves of books have been written. Countless photographs have been snapped. At Churchill Downs there's a whole museum dedicated to the race. There can be no doubt: The Kentucky Derby is the biggest of them all.

Tell someone you've been, and they lean in and brighten up. It's the only race that will have that effect on everyone. A horseplayer or fan will listen to track talk about any race, but try telling someone who doesn't follow racing that you went to the Travers and they'll ask you what it is. Tell them you went to the Derby and they'll be impressed.

I believe there is confusion about the Derby scene. Some folks imagine that the Derby takes place on a big green lawn, that servants attend you, that icy juleps are slipped into your hand by stealthy waiters in white topcoats, that the women are demure smiling belles while the men are preening, seersuckered dandies and stern old colonels. Others think it's a Mardi Gras party, bare boobies everywhere, crazy crackers reeling around, spilling whiskey and vomiting on the their shoes while irresponsible gamblers put up the deed to the house on a long shot. It is, of course, all of these things and none of them.

This is national mythology we're into. The Derby is like George Washington's cherry tree, only it happens every year. Other sporting events are bigger. There's more money gambled on the Super Bowl, but the Super Bowl is a different animal. It's a game with teams and fans. In horse racing, no one's a fan of anything except a good overlay, when the chances of a horse winning a race are much better than his odds, usually because of a hyped favorite. This isn't an Army-Navy game or a cold night at Lambeau Field. This is a party, a day, a festival, a legend.

It's also an incredible hassle. Here's the truth: the party is middling fun. There are mint juleps aplenty, and I love them, but you can do that at home. The rumored depravity in the infield pales in comparison to a raucous night at a good party or a cheap bar. Sure, there's mud wrestling, and flashes of skin, and beer everywhere, but it's a rather tame experience. A lot of families out there are just milling around. A lot of pitiful folks drunk for the first time since the last wedding they went to are bending elbows with some self-congratulatory (We Party!) college kids who are thoroughly reasonable when it comes right down to it, and much too law-abiding to start the kind of trouble that warrants the reputation the Derby has developed.

Not that the party isn't out of control: it is. But it's off the hook precisely because of the innocence of the partiers. Like

Bourbon Street, prom night, or office Christmas parties, the Kentucky Derby is an excuse. There's something sad and underwhelming about amateur night. Give me a roadhouse filled with bikers and foxhunters (the two craziest demographics I've ever seen).

Somewhere in one of the large buildings devoted to plush hospitality, very famous, very rich, and very thin folks are hanging around a bar absolutely creaking under the weight of the champagne, while platters of cold shrimp, each the size of a parakeet, are rushed to the sideboard. But these luxurious cells aren't accessible to anyone, and the swells pretty much stay there, occasionally drifting to the terrace to look out on the swarming masses. The buildings in which these wonderful moments of Louisville hospitality take place look like concrete public housing developments. They are huge and unwelcoming, as far from gentility as can be imagined. One is reminded constantly that Louisville is not, in fact, the South, but a sort of blend of South and Midwest. Churchill Downs isn't subtle or elegant. It is relentlessly renovated, and most of the renovations have been accomplished in the stadium style. Boring, practical, concrete attempts at managing an unmanageable crowd, with no nod to historical preservation. One of the press officers there told me once that he was pretty sure there was a betting window in the building left over from a nineteenth-century renovation. "Yeah, I think they sell ice cream out of it."

For civilians—those who are not locked into the luxury cells above or who have no access to the wonderful press annex with its buffet, bar, and betting windows—it's difficult to place a bet or get a hot dog. When your friend goes to place a bet, he'll be gone an hour and a half.

Truckloads of bloated, squinting, drunken fools are carted off to jail in plastic riot handcuffs by the end of the day. I once saw a woman with a big gorgeous hat, dressed to the nines in a white church suit, teetering drunkenly and leaning against a concrete pillar. She had wrapped herself in a clear trash bag against the rain and had her white shoes in the hand that supported her, dangling in her fingers from the leather straps. She was picking a large piece of broken glass out of her foot.

I've seen a couple, a grown man and woman, respectable folks who on any other day must get up early to go to work, reduced and degraded until they looked like bums. The two had set up a litter in between two trash cans, against a cold cinderblock wall. The trash cans were overflowing with race programs and beer cans, sticky mint julep juice trickling down their sides. The couple had covered the floor with newspaper. He was smoking a stub of a cigar, and she had her stained, tissue-thin blue dress tucked up luridly between her knees. They had about a dozen empty plastic cocktail glasses around them, and another dozen cans of beer. They were intently reading the race program, muttering to one another with marked hostility. It was 2 P.M.

It's a depressing, maddening scene. For most of the day you wonder why you came.

Then everything changes. The ninth race, the Woodford Reserve Turf Classic, is suddenly over and a wave of realization washes over all of Churchill Downs: the next race is the Kentucky Derby. In 2004, Stroll cantered home two and a half

They're off! at the Kentucky Derby.

lengths out front over a very soft turf course to win the slowest Woodford Reserve ever. He finished the nine furlongs in 1:53 flat.

That's it. The next race run will be the Kentucky Derby.

Even the laughable aspects shine: 150,000 people muddle through the words of "My Old Kentucky Home." Everyone stands up on the seats, straining to see the track. You must stand on your seat too, or you won't see a thing. It is suddenly astonishingly crowded. You thought it was crowded ten minutes ago, but now everyone at the track is thinking the same thing. A single-purpose crowd is not sustainable, but it is fabulous for a little while.

The air sparkles with electricity. Again, all considerations such as the weather and one's mood and the rest of the racing day vanish. Your brain is flooded with new glucose, and your focus is brilliant and tight. Your eyes become like telephoto lenses. It's an all-encompassing, totally absorbing moment. It's too big to be true, but it is true. You're about to see the Kentucky Derby.

When the starting gate flies open, the crowd roars like nothing you've ever heard, and you have goose bumps. You'll want to kiss the person standing next to you.

Three weeks later you'll forget the rest of the day, all the hassle, the crazy mess that is Derby Day. But you'll remember with crystal clarity that moment when the green gate slammed open and a huge field of the best three-year-olds in the country did that wonderful two-footed leap to start their run. You'll remember when they went off.

In the *New York Times* in 1985, Whitney Tower wrote one of the best Kentucky Derby pieces I've ever read. At the time he was the president of the National Museum of Racing. His piece begins: "Every year, it's the same wretched predicament. I walk out of that ramshackle wreck known as Churchill Downs after 10 or 12 hours reporting or just plain living through the events of a Kentucky Derby, and as I trudge in the darkness through and over broken glass, mounds of paper and the occasional groaning body toward the parking lot, I say to myself—sometimes even out loud for the ghosts of derbies past to hear—I will never go through such a rat race again in my life. I swear it. So here I am, packing once more for the trip to Louisville."

THE DERBY wasn't always such a big deal. It wasn't exactly small beer, but once upon a time it was a regional race, one among many. It was Colonel Matt Winn, who stood in the infield at the very first Derby in 1875 (then saw every one until 1949), who turned it into the Derby we know today. He bought Churchill Downs with a consortium of friends in 1902, and instigated a huge run of publicity and marketing to make the Run for the Roses the most important race in America. He is the father of the modern Kentucky Derby, but it's not his race.

It was another Kentucky Colonel who founded the race, one whose name takes a little more buffing to make it shine—not that various histories haven't been happy to provide.

In the wonderful antique book titled *The American Turf,* edited by Lymon Weeks, one reads: "One of the notable army of American turfmen that performed such a great work for the cause of racing in the Untied States in the years immediately following the close of the Civil War, was Colonel M. Lewis Clark, of Kentucky. For more than a third of a century he has been one of the most conspicuous figures in American turf history. His career is worthy of particular attention for the reason that he entered upon the work of developing the turf at a time when and in a section of the country where the situation was very discouraging." Racing in the South, even in neutral Kentucky, was at what *The American Turf* rather delicately calls a "low ebb." And quite a problem it was for the Southerners, too, who still loved their horses but had "little means and little disposition to indulge in the sport."

Louisville itself was in pretty fair shape, it seems. The big river and the railhead made the city strategically vital during the war. "I may have God on my side," Lincoln was reported to have said, "but I must have Kentucky."

While Louisville had been spared, horse country had not. Federal troops had razed the plantations; bands of outlaws had raided the stud farms. Southern blood horses, which had sold for thousands before the war, were now going for $150.

On June 22, 1874, the Galt House hotel, right on the Ohio River, hosted the first meeting of the Louisville Jockey Club and Driving Park Association. The businessmen, bankers, and thoroughbred breeders signed articles of incorporation, and Meriwether Lewis Clark, Jr., was appointed president.

This was no surprise. Young "Lutie," as he was known, had been groomed for the job.

Lutie was born on January 27, 1846, at Spring Grove Plantation. His grandfather was William Clark, co-leader of the Lewis and Clark expedition. M. L. Clark, Sr., was a West Point graduate who served in the Civil War and the Mexican War as an engineer. He later was commandant of cadets and professor of higher mathematics at the Kentucky Military Institute. He married Abigail Churchill, a daughter of one of Kentucky's first families. Clark Sr. seems to have been a rather neglectful spouse, preferring military life to the softer pleasures of the home. He did hang around enough to get seven children by Abigail. She died after the birth of her seventh, and Clark sent his children to live with various members of the family. Lutie ended up at the home of two unmarried brothers, his uncles John and William Henry Churchill.

The Churchill boys were very rich and figured very highly in Louisville society. They were sharp dressers, alluring figures.

Lutie was a welcome addition to their home on Sixth Street. They taught him to appreciate bespoke suits, champagne, leisure, and horse racing.

Most of what's written on Lutie is quite flattering. A little reading between the lines, however, reveals that he was essentially a trust-fund brat with a temper like a gasoline fire. At college in Bardstown, Kentucky, he showed little enthusiasm for education. He avoided service in the Civil War. He worked, but not very hard, at banking. The Churchill boys sent him on a Grand Tour in 1867. He stayed in Europe for a few months, taking advantage of the hospitality of exiled Confederate general John C. Breckinridge. Breckinridge had been our youngest vice president of the United States under Buchanan. He rode in battle as a division commander of the famed Orphan Brigade, a group of Kentucky confederates. Shortly before Richmond fell, he fled to Cuba, then to Europe to avoid the charge of treason. Breckinridge was also a fan of horses off the battlefield. With Breckinridge as a host, Lutie was in good shape.

Lutie returned to Kentucky and embarked on a very casual career in tobacco, his every move eased by his uncles. In 1872 he traveled again to Europe, this time to study the races there. He stayed with Admiral John Henry Rous, head of the English Jockey Club. Lutie went to the Epsom Derby and liked the race, though at the time it was famously corrupt. At Longchamps, in Paris, he discovered the machines that Pierre Oller had built in 1865 to rid the racing world of bookmakers. Oller's *mutuel* machines allowed bettors to wager among themselves, with the Jockey Club taking a vig right out of the pot. Lutie shipped four of the machines home and installed one of them in the lobby of the Galt House. He hoped that people would become accustomed to it.

For Lutie was a man with a mission. His second trip to Europe had not been for pleasure. Louisville needed a track.

Lutie's pitch was a hard one: Build a dream of a track. Offer races like the Epsom Derby, and the Oaks, and the English Classics. Use the new *mutuel* machines. A winner of the new Kentucky Derby, Lutie prophesied, would be worth more than the farm upon which it had been born. *Turf, Field and Farm* quoted Lutie in 1897 as saying that "one offspring of a Kentucky Derby winner would fetch more as a yearling than did his dam and the dam of his sire combined." The prediction, they wrote, had been realized.

Lutie sold 320 shares of stock in the new Louisville Jockey Club for a hundred dollars each. The Jockey Club ran out of money before the track was built, but the Churchill boys kicked in more. Still, the new park resorted to deadbeating a few of its contractors.

It is clear that the Churchill boys wanted this track. They had many friends who were losing money in the horse business. They gave a lot of money to the enterprise. But always, in their dealings with Lutie, it seems as if they didn't really trust him.

Consider the location. The track was built on the Churchills' land, but they didn't give Lutie a nice swath of green hilltop. They gave him a swamp, crawling with mudbugs, swarming with mosquitoes. The land was unusable. Lucky Lutie, it turned out. The swampland makes for good drainage. To this day the oval at Churchill Downs recovers from a heavy rain more quickly than most tracks.

By the mid 1880s, Lutie was riding high. He would throw lavish Derby breakfasts at the private Pendennis Club (founded, in part, by the Churchill boys). His meals were famous. At one dinner the guests sat at tables drawn together in a giant circle, surrounding a reproduced country pond, complete with fountain, moss, and ducklings. Another dinner was held around a detailed model of the track, with wooden horses and brightly painted jockeys arranged as they had run that afternoon.

On his way to Churchill Downs from the club in the morning, Lynne Renau writes in her *Jockeys, Belles, and Bluegrass Kings*, Lutie would lug his three hundred pounds up into the Louisville Jockey Club carriage, a polished, gleaming, red tally-ho vehicle drawn by four high-stepping bays. You can imagine him, shooting the cuffs of his handmade shirt, smoothing the fabric of his custom-tailored suit with yellow kid gloves. He set his hat and urged the four bays on their way with a flick of the reins.

The clubhouse he built was described in the *Louisville Herald Post* in 1934: "There was loveliness surrounding the old clubhouse, more mellowness and charm. It's wide verandas and spacious rooms were appointed like those of a private club, which indeed it was. . . . In the cool shade of the overspreading trees, you saw white-coated Negroes passing from the house to groups on the lawn, bearing trays of frosted silver goblets crowned with sprigs of mint."

Lutie's Derby is the Derby of the imagination. He was exorbitant, extravagant, and wild. Typical of his enthusiasm was the short-lived Moet & Chandon Stakes, after which the winner was obliged to buy four cases of champagne for the Jockey Club, to be consumed on the spot. The champagne cost more than the purse of the race. Lutie would mix mint juleps in giant cups to be passed from guest to guest. He would bring in the beautiful, the famous, the rich, and treat them royally. He had really done it: his dream had become a reality.

But it was doomed.

As wild as he was, Lutie never gambled on horses. He was doctrinaire in his pursuit of rectitude at the racetrack, and his sense of right was followed up with personal force.

In 1879, Lutie got into it with T. G. Moore, a breeder and owner. Lutie said Moore's entry fees were past due and refused to let him race. Moore demanded an apology; he'd been racing in Kentucky since Lutie was in short pants. Lutie knocked him to the floor of his Galt House office and held a gun on him, demanding his departure from the premises.

Moore returned and shot Lutie in the chest through the door. Lutie was fine.

Lutie was now in demand throughout the racing world. He was the impresario of what would soon be called Churchill Downs, after all, and as such he traveled to Chicago and worked at Garfield Park racetrack for an outrageous one hundred dollars per day (something like eighteen hundred dollars in today's money). In return for his stewardship there, he also received a carriage to and from his hotel, where he ate sumptuously at a private table lit by an antique chandelier, its candles covered by pink shades. All his expenses were paid by the track.

One night he groused that Chicagoans were thieves and liars. A fight with the bartender ensued, and Lutie stormed off. When he reappeared, he put a revolver to his adversary's chest and demanded an apology.

Lutie was a whirlwind. He even finagled a brief position as parks commissioner in Louisville. In retrospect it's clear he had one thing in mind: the widening of the road to Churchill Downs. He left the city with a bill for twenty thousand dollars' worth of road construction.

Meanwhile Lutie's uncles had remarried, and one of them had produced an heir. Lutie was no longer the sole male descendant. And his uncles were getting sick of him.

First, Henry gave his brother John the land that held the racetrack, and didn't even mention Lutie in his will. In John's will, the money Lutie had once assumed would be his own went to the wife. By 1884, Lutie must have known he was cut off.

The Jockey Club finances too were slipping.

There were disagreements with the starters, disagreements with the bookmakers, and disagreements with the horsemen.

One of the premier Kentucky breeders, the fabulously wealthy Ben Ali Haggin, got into a squabble with one of Lutie's officials over a bookmaker strike and shipped his horses back to New York. Haggin was an influential man, and Peter Chew quotes Colonel Matt Winn saying that what resulted from that walkout in 1886 was "something equivalent to a boycott of Churchill Downs by eastern horse owners. . . . No eastern owners of high class three-year-olds—except Mike Dwyer in 1896—sent their horses to the Kentucky Derby Post for over a quarter of a century."

In the Panic of 1893, Lutie lost a bundle in the stock market. He hung on to the Jockey Club until the summer of 1894, but by then his club was broke, his track needed improvements, and he was having a hard time climbing stairs. The track was sold to a consortium of bookmakers calling themselves the New Louisville Jockey Club. They built the twin spires that are Churchill Downs's trademark.

Lutie took to wandering. He worked at tracks in Mexico, Nashville, Texas. In 1897, in another Wall Street crash, Lutie lost yet more money, as did many horsemen. Tracks were closed; horses were sold.

In the spring of 1899, Lutie was working at a track in Memphis. On April 22 he sat his huge body down on his hotel bed, put a pistol to his head, and pulled the trigger.

THE HORSES that did not run the Derby can be an interesting list: Man o' War, Seabiscuit, Cigar—many of the best never made the trip for one reason or another. This in no way diminishes the list of the greats that dashed under the wire. Exterminator, Zev, Black Gold, Swaps, Northern Dancer, Riva Ridge, Spectacular Bid—these are racing greats, giants of the sport. There are also the eleven Triple Crown winners, all of which ran around the track at Churchill Downs on their journey to racing history. So many excellent races have been run on the first Saturday in May that it is almost impossible to decide which are the most elucidating or entertaining.

Secretariat, in 1973, rolled from the back of the pack and ran each section of the race faster than the one before. He ran like a horse of a different breed altogether, slamming home in record time, three lengths faster than Northern Dancer had run it. His record still stands. What a race.

Stevie Cauthen was all of eighteen when he won the Derby on Affirmed. He'd won more money as an apprentice jockey than anyone ever had, and he'd been a pro since he was sixteen. And even though he had just ridden one of the best racehorses ever to hit the track to a wild victory, with Alydar closing like a swinging door behind them, he looked like an elf child, a sweet, big-eyed American boy.

Aristedes was entered in the first Derby as a speed horse, a rabbit to set the race up for his stablemate, but he just ran away with it, and so began a tradition of unpredictability that continues to this day.

The famed jockey Bill Shoemaker stood up on Gallant Man while half a furlong from the finish, thinking he'd won the race. His horse slowed, and Iron Leige got by him for the win.

But the best Derby story, to my mind, comes in 1933.

The governor of Kentucky, Ruby Laffoon, gave a short speech to the press before the race, which began: "Mint Juleps are not what they used to be in Kentucky." It had been thirteen years since bourbon and minted simple syrup were legally poured over crushed ice. I think the governor must have felt it deeply: he was battling an economic crisis so severe that he closed the banks and tobacco markets that year. There was the faint promise of a New Deal program that might bail Kentucky out, but the state couldn't scrape up the matching funds. "But thank God we have beautiful women

and Kentucky thoroughbreds still left." Laffoon was entertaining the president's son, James Roosevelt.

The previous night had been rainy, and the clouds stayed
on through the day. It was cool and breezy. The track was listed
as "good" (which would more aptly be called "good enough";
a track that is good for running is called "fast").

The night had seen at least one major change in the
thirteen-horse field. Head Play, at the seventh post, had
changed owners only the day before. Peter Chew writes:
"Head Play was owned by Willie Crump, an old-time retired
jockey who had picked him up as a yearling for $500 and had
developed into one of the nation's top two-year-olds of 1932.
Not long before the Derby, Mrs. Silas B. Mason offered
Crump $30,000 and 15 percent of any part of the Derby purse
that Head Play won." Crump deliberated, but he finally sold.

The favorite was a joint entry from W. R. Coe, Ladysman
and Pomponious. They went off at about 3-2.

Head Play acted up on reaching the starting gate, which
was a clumsy-looking thing out of which the horses stuck
halfway; only their rumps were actually in the gate. Two
horses, from the newsreel footage I have of the race, seem to
start from outside the gate. The official chart says the start was
good for all, which is partly true. Herb Fisher took Head Play
up on the pace, quickly, and he tucked in behind the early
speed. The duelers out front were Good Advice and Isaiah.
Those three got off well. The rest of the horses bumped and
smashed their way down to the clubhouse turn.

It is an incredible traffic jam. Every horse in the field
bumps every other horse, and they look, for a moment, like

some kind of kinetic manifestation of a medieval painting, back when the painters just saw a field of color and a bunch of feet, instead of individuated forms. About seventy yards out from the gate, that's what the field looked like, just a mass of horse, with a couple of heads and forty feet. Don Meade, up on Brokers Tip, would no doubt agree with the chart and say that he pulled his horse and settled in at the back of the pack, avoiding the traffic on the stretch. He had little choice in the matter. The field squeezed Brokers Tip to the back of the pack like squeezing a tomato from its skin. He settled and hit the first turn running well.

After a respectable half-mile, Good Advice and Isaiah setting fractions of 23-1/5 and 47-1/5, Fisher asked Head Play to run, and he quickly dispatched the two rabbits. Head Play was running strong on the lead, but his first challenge was coming. Charlie Corbett spurred Charley O. They moved forward on the inside. The two who had led were running last and eleventh, destroyed and exhausted, plodding along with their ears laid down as if they were wearing cinderblocks for shoes. They were spent after only three-quarters of a mile.

At the far turn, Head Play had held on to his lead. He had a length over Charley O.

Brokers Tip had been picking off horses. Running in the great Derby style, the dramatic move from last that is the telltale sign of a classic distance horse. He moved up into striking position and tried to run inside and save ground around the turn, but he hit interference. Another squash of horse traffic was bumping around the second turn. Meade drove him toward the rail, and by the end of the turn they were sitting tight.

[65]

One of the best moments in any race, but especially at a big one, is when the horses snap out of that turn and use all they've got left for the stretch. The announcer hollers, "And the field turns for home!" The roar rises from the crowd.

When the runners hit the stretch, Fisher swung Head Play wide, pushing Charley O out. Meade and Brokers Tip were flying now. They were on the inside, and threatening. Briefly it looked as if the duel to the wire would be among three hard-charging horses, but Charley O had no more. He faded. Fisher steered Head Play back toward the rail. Head Play and Brokers Tip were flat out. Both horses were running well, low to the ground. They devoured the stretch. Both jocks were driving hard. They buried their faces in the manes of their mounts, each step, each gust of wind pushed the mane back across their cheek. They brushed their hands on the necks of the horses and flashed their whips.

At that moment the Kentucky Derby became a rodeo. First, Fisher leaned down and grabbed at Meade's saddlecloth. Meade shoved Fisher's hand clear. The jockeys were whipping the hell out of their horses, and it's clear that more than a couple cracks of Meade's stick hit Fisher. Fisher leaned in, taking his right foot out of the stirrup, and grabbed at the cloth again. His right knee was poking into the air. He was wobbling along atop his galloping horse.

It's difficult enough to maintain balance on a charging thoroughbred. Jockeys make it look like the easiest thing in the world to teeter on the balls of your feet, the stirrups' thin strips of metal supporting all your weight, while only your calves make contact with the barrel of this surging beast.

The famous fighting finish of the 1933 Kentucky Derby, jockeys Herb Fisher and Don Meade up.

Now Fisher only had one foot in. He yanked the reins. Head Play's head jerked to the right. The horses flashed across the finish line so close together that the crowd couldn't tell which horse had won.

Fisher's yank of the reins, jerking Head Play's head, had cost him the race. Brokers Tip had won it by a nose.

Damon Runyon wrote about the race in the *Courier-Journal*:

When Fisher brought Head Play back to the finish, and dismounted, he immediately ran, with little short jiggly steps in his riding boots, across the lawn to the stewards stand to lodge a claim of foul against Meade.

[67]

Fisher broke down and cried as he talked to the stewards. Meantime, however, they had already drooped the neck of Brokers Tip with a rose blanket, and had handed Meade a big bunch of American Beauties, and the photographers were busy taking pictures of the horse.

The crowd waited anxiously while the stewards heard Fisher's case. Hundreds were out on the track, scurrying under the feet of the horses of the mounted policemen. . . . Presently, the red "official" board went up and the result passed into history.

According to Peter Chew, Fisher cried again upon leaving the stewards. He then composed himself and dashed to the jockey's room to fight Meade.

There are two photos that communicate more about racing than any others I've seen. In the first one a horse is actually biting another horse in the middle of a race, trying to keep the challenger from passing him. The other is a photo snapped by newspaper photographer Wallace Lowry, who was lying under the rail on the inside of the track snapping pictures as fast as he could. The whole thing was over in a flash, and the horses were flying along at forty miles per hour, but he got the shot. He caught the two jocks locked in a fistfight in the final yards of the 1933 Kentucky Derby.

4
Racing as It Should Be

T horoughbreds took to the Bluegrass region of Kentucky as if they'd lived there forever, as if they were designed to live there. How could Kentucky not always have been home to these horses? How could there have been a time before miles of expensive painted fences demarcated the land and set the slopes alive in beautiful geometry?

The first time—and the ninetieth time—you see a spring foal standing against his mother in a field behind a white fence, with a building in the background that looks like a cross between a cathedral and a barn (certainly it isn't just some place to throw hay), it will stop you in your tracks. You'll stare at this picture that you've seen on postcards and in paintings. You'll take very treacly photographs. I've filled up rolls of film with useless snapshots suitable for the dust jackets of books written for twelve-year-old girls. Four horses cavorting by a tree on a hill in the Bluegrass. Sunset, foal, fence.

The cliché does not diminish the view. Conformation is a term used by horsemen to describe the ratios and proportions of how a horse is put together. The diagrams drawn to map out the perfect thoroughbred look just like Leonardo's famous drawing of a man. When you see thoroughbreds in a pasture in the central Bluegrass, the whole scene is perfectly conformed. These ratios, these proportions, this sunlight, that grass, that horse, that fence: all were made for one another. When you see it, you feel it has always been so.

Looking at the youngest crop on a horse farm in the Bluegrass, with the perfectly conformed landscape, there is an added fascination that the foal at his dam's flank behind the slats of the fences of one of the world's finest stud farms—maybe it's an old Kentucky farm, maybe it's owned by a Saudi Arabian prince, maybe it's an extension of an Irish stud farm—is a promising young horse. This is Lexington, Kentucky, and there are no foals without promise in these parts. These are the racehorses that will run the Kentucky Derby. One of these horses will win the Blue Grass Stakes at Keeneland.

Horses used to run in Lexington at the Kentucky Association track, built in 1826 to replace tracks that dated from the late 1700s. It was located in the center of town, which in turn was the center of the Bluegrass horse country, which made it probably the horsiest track in the world.

The Keeneland Association replaced the Kentucky Association in 1936. Its two short race meets are packed with good races, but the biggest race run there is the Blue Grass Stakes.

On April 27, 1978, a horse named Alydar had a saddle thrown over his big chestnut back in Keeneland's leafy paddock for the fifty-sixth running of the Blue Grass Stakes. After an excellent two-year-old career in which he'd notched the only defeat handed to his rival Affirmed, Alydar had wintered in Florida. His trainer John Veitch had spent his time at Hialeah wondering if Alydar was nothing more than a precocious colt. Over the winter there is always the fear that other colts will grow and mature while your Derby dream horse will turn out to be a plodder. But at Hialeah on February 11, 1978, Alydar had romped to an easy victory, going seven furlongs. Then he won the Flamingo Stakes by four and a half lengths. Alydar next took the Florida Derby by two lengths and came back to Kentucky looking very good. He had one more prep before the Kentucky Derby, the Blue Grass Stakes. It seemed that all he had on the line was whether or not he'd be the favorite on the first Saturday in May.

Nine horses went to the post for the Blue Grass, each of them absurdly outgunned by Alydar. Some 22,000 people were on hand, and all of them knew it was Alydar's race. Alydar was a local favorite, and the people at Keeneland know their local horses.

Discovering Keeneland is akin to discovering that someone in your family owns a horse farm. Anyone like me, who learned about tracks at Belmont, Aqueduct, Gulfstream, and Hialeah, will not immediately recognize this as a place for horse racing. The grandstand looks more like a library at a fine private school. The grounds are trimmed and lush. Everything is built out of stone. The paddock is a lawn party among the hedges, with light white lawn furniture and a rock wall. At Keeneland even the parking lots are pretty. Nowhere to be seen are the typical oceans of asphalt that surround most tracks. Keeneland's parking lot is woodier than most parks. Plenty of old trees shade the cars and dapple the sunlight.

Keeneland Race Course in Lexington, Kentucky.

At the gate stands a post from the old Kentucky Association with "KA" carved onto the top, which stands now for Keeneland Association and serves to dedicate the track to the history of Lexington racing. History is cherished at Keeneland. The best horse-racing library is there, in another beautiful stone building up on a hill. For years they ran races without a public address system. It wasn't installed until 1997—the idea being that the people who watch races here know what's going on. They don't need help figuring it out.

The whole track is made to feel as if it has sat on this hill forever, as if buglers have been calling horses to the post at least since 1650.

Kentuckians, it seems to me, have the same feeling as a visitor to the Bluegrass. They too feel that this place must have been always as it is now. They know it's not true, and they demonstrate a deep anxiety about creating the illusion of historical provenance. The hardboots and bluebloods of Kentucky would love to rewrite history so that when Daniel Boone hit their state he was astride a thoroughbred. Having established that, they would set to work proving that the cave paintings in Lascaux were in fact pictographs of Kentucky blood horses drawn on good old Kentucky limestone and exported to France.

It's an understandable fancy, and it's one that is supported when a great-looking horse like Alydar shows up. Not just because he was the big horse, a popular star of the track, but because he was the latest—and would prove to be the last—in a long line of champions sent to the post from Calumet Farm, just about a mile up the road from Keeneland.

When John Veitch gave jockey Jorge Velasquez a leg up, and the bugler blew his call to the post, they were participating in more than the fifty-sixth running of the Blue Grass Stakes, more than a great stakes race, more than a Kentucky Derby prep. As the nine horses went to the post, they were participating in one of racing's diamonds, an incredible compression of history and sensibility. For Alydar was Calumet Farm's last big horse, running at Keeneland in the Blue Grass Stakes, and it just doesn't get any more poignant than that.

Calumet, like Keeneland, is another piece of Kentucky that seems retroactively eternal. After it came to be, how could it not always have been?

WILLIAM WRIGHT founded the farm in 1924 after he made a lot of money hustling Calumet baking powder. He sent salesmen into the field to conduct in-home demonstrations, all of them claiming that egg whites in the powder made the stuff more effective. The sales tactic worked, and William Wright moved his farm from Illinois to Kentucky, just outside Lexington.

When William's son Warren Wright, Sr., took it over, he kicked things into gear. He sold the baking powder company to General Foods for forty million dollars and got down to seriously breeding and racing thoroughbreds.

Calumet Farm's first big horse was Nellie Flag, in 1934, a granddaughter of Man o' War and the best two-year-old running. She was the favorite in the 1935 Kentucky Derby, where she was the first Derby mount for the young Eddie Arcaro. (He would go on to win five Derbies, but not that one—that race belonged to Omaha.)

In 1936, Wright joined A. B. Hancock, Sr., in a syndicate to import a stallion named Blenheim II, and bought a yearling named Bull Lea. These two horses would establish a bloodline for Calumet that may very well be unmatched. Each of the two foundation stallions gave Calumet a Triple Crown winner. Whirlaway was a son of Bleinheim II, and Citation was the son of Bull Lea.

Winning 18 percent of all the Triple Crowns ever won is pretty good shakes already, but Calumet's accomplishments don't stop there. Twelve times Calumet has been the winningest owner when the yearly money count is figured. Eleven years in a row they were the leading American breeder. Nineteen horses owned by Calumet have won thirty-eight divisional or Horse of the Year championships. Calumet-bred horses have won the Kentucky Derby nine times; eight of them were owned by the farm. They have bred and owned seven winners of the Preakness Stakes. The Calumet silks, Devil Red with blue hoops, have become famous. The farm itself, with its miles of white fences and all its barns painted red and white, has become the geographical manifestation of horse racing.

The forties belonged to Calumet. I can't imagine anyone has seen anything like the concentrated, brilliant domination that began in 1940, when Whirlaway drifted out coming around his first stretch turn—a crazy habit that would be fixed with intensive training and a custom-made one-eyed blinker—and won his race anyway. Calumet ran so many good horses in these years that huge stakes winners would basically be the stablemate, second-stringers behind Calumet champions.

Calumet closed out the forties with Citation. It was the first horse to give Man o' War's reputation a run for its money, certainly one of the top three racehorses of all time, called by Eddie Arcaro "The runningest son of a bitch I ever been on."

When Warren Wright, Sr., died in 1950, he was survived by his wife Lucille. His obituary in the *Thoroughbred Record* read: "He played the game the way all games should be played, with a fierce devotion to the main objective, content with nothing but paramount achievement. . . . The devil red, not merely the symbol of the ultimate aristocracy of the Turf, became also the proud banner of the $2 bettor. They believed in it, and they worshipped the horses that bore it."

Calumet didn't die with Warren Wright, Sr., but things changed.

Lucille met and married Admiral Gene Markey, Hollywood playboy, bon vivant, and writer. He took to Kentucky

Aerial view of Calumet Farm, an icon of the sport.

like a fish to water. At Calumet the parties got bigger, the friends and visitors more glamorous. The farm took on a humorous air under the Markeys. They made a Christmas card of the two of them selling lemonade by the giant wrought-iron gates of the farm, under the shade of an umbrella held over their heads by their servant Charles Rankin, with a sign that read "Calumet must survive." It's a classic of the Markey era.

But they weren't joking about horse racing. The famous Calumet trophy room continued to be filled with gold and silver.

And they weren't joking about money. Warren Wright, Sr., had set up the operation seemingly airtight, and the farm was debt free. They were raking it in.

By 1978, though, the Markeys were not well. They didn't go to the races anymore. The Calumet silks were still seen at the track, and in the winner's circle, but there hadn't been a really big horse in a while. Lucille Markey loved Alydar, and clearly he was the last big horse the Markeys would have. He was Lucille Markey's favorite, perhaps. She named him after their friend the Aly Kahn, whom she called Aly Darling. "Aly Daaahhhhling!"

Without Ted Bassett, the president of Keeneland, the Markeys might not have seen the Blue Grass Stakes. He took the track station wagon a mile up the road to Calumet, got the Markeys into it—both of them failing, arthritic, weak—and drove them back to Keeneland. He drove the wagon right up to the rail on the stretch turn and parked it there. The Markeys could watch the race and listen to the call on the car radio.

For the post parade they walked slowly to the edge of the track and leaned on the rail. Gene was in tweed, with a houndstooth cap and a red neck scarf; Lucille was in blue with white gloves.

John Veitch, Alydar's trainer, wrote in *The Blood Horse,* "As the post parade moved near the Markeys, jockey Jorge Velasquez brought Alydar close to his lady." Lucille, the grand dame of the Kentucky turf, got to see her best baby race-ready once more. "Stopping, the horse placed his right foot forward and dropped his head, bowing in respect."

Velasquez, Alydar, Bassett—everyone was playing along to give this moment to the Markeys. Everyone was giving them a chance to appreciate one more big horse in what had been, especially for Mrs. Markey, an incredible string of them.

Then the Markeys went back to the car and the horses went to the gate. Alydar's odds were 1-10.

At the start, Alydar was caught off guard. He wasn't ready, and the start surprised him. Instead of the firm good push that sets a horse right where he wants to be, Alydar lunged from the gate. Velasquez gave the colt some rein and Alydar settled within a few lengths. Once he hit his stride, Velasquez settled him well off the pace. They sat tight.

Veitch later said the track was heavy that day, though it was listed as "fast." Raymond Earl went to the lead and pulled the field through honest fractions. He began to open it up. Raymond Earl was running good. Up on Alydar, Velasquez was getting nervous. On the backstretch, Raymond Earl had five lengths of daylight opened up.

That's a metaphor—daylight—that's especially suitable to Keeneland racing. The clubhouse faces west, into the afternoon sun. The crowd watching the horses across the infield has to squint to see them. This is because no afternoon racing was supposed to take place at Keeneland when it was originally designed.

JACK KEENE, whose Keeneland stud farm would eventually become the site of this pastoral racetrack, was an adventurous, passionate horseman. Throughout even the glossiest accounts, his career seems tinged with a kind of mild insanity of exuberance. He trained horses in England, Ireland, Japan, and Russia. In Russia for the seasons of 1902 and 1903, he won every major stakes race that was run. In one three-month period he won 116 races. The Russians accused him of doping his horses. He said it was the shoes he used, which were lighter and gave him the edge over the rough iron that the Russians used for shodding. The Russian equivalent to the Jockey Club rewrote the rules to exclude foreigners from stakes races. Keene shrugged it off.

A couple of years later, he and a small stable were embarked on a steamer en route to Japan to enter the Japan Derby. He was quarantined with his horses at a beach until a few days before the race. No oval to train on, no furlong markers, no track kitchen, but no matter—his horses finished one, two in the Derby. He claimed: "That beach was the best track I ever trained over."

He did finally settle down in the Bluegrass and raced his horses at the old Kentucky Association. And he immediately began dreaming up new tracks. He started on one at Keeneland Stud in 1916 so that horses could be seen in their natural environment. What better place to watch a horse race than on a horse farm?

Next Keene built a mile oval called Raceland on 350 acres near a town then known as Chinnville, and opened it in 1924. He filled the infield with honeysuckle, bridle paths, flowers, a lake, and gardens. He ran promotions: a boxing match on July Fourth, opening day on July 10. He threw a Ladies Day and an Ashland Day, named after the biggest proximate city. On July 19 he staged the inaugural running of the Raceland Derby, with that year's Kentucky Derby winner Black Gold, owned by Rosa Hoots and trained by Hanly Webb, the heavily bet favorite.

In 1928, Raceland was lost. The plant was hundreds of thousands of dollars in debt, owed back taxes, and was heavily mortgaged. A circuit court judge ordered that the track be auctioned, and the "million dollar oval" was sold for $45,000 and destroyed. Today there's a driving range on the site and, as of May 2004, a commemorative marker.

This loss must have bothered Jack Keene, but he seems to have been now enraptured with his own two-decade project: the obsessive, extravagant construction of the track at Keeneland Stud.

At the close of the eighteenth century, Patrick Henry had granted about eight thousand acres of land to Francis Keen (Jack's great-great-grandfather). Only one small parcel of the land had ever left the family, and that was bought back pretty quickly. All they changed was the spelling of their name. Some thought "Keen" was too plain, others apparently that "Keene" was ostentatious. All the while they had bred horses on the land.

Keene wanted horses to race there for the pure sport of it. In the book published to celebrate the opening of Keeneland, George B. "Brownie" Leach wrote that Keene's dream was to make a place "where friends could gather and match their horses, free from undesirable phases of the sport."

If you squint, you can see that what's at work here is a deep-seated desire to keep horse racing among the horse set. Like a chef standing in the kitchen complaining that if all these customers would just go away he'd be able to get some work done, some factions of horse racing believe that all these fans, touts, bookmakers, and turf writers just get in the way.

Keene's track was eight and a half furlongs, and though he'd worked hard to grade and bank it, and many "experts" proclaimed it among the finest in the land, it nonetheless dipped more than a dozen feet on the backstretch. Still, the track was a pretty good one.

The clubhouse was grand. Keene had built a combination home, barn, and clubhouse with stalls for a dozen horses, a ballroom, sleeping quarters, and a fireplace that could burn a six-foot log. The garage had room for twenty cars. Keene had some heavy fun in mind. He wanted his friends to be able to come and watch races in the morning, eat, and then dance the night away. The clubhouse was built facing west because he never thought he'd run a race in the afternoon.

All the buildings were of stone quarried from Keene's own land. Apparently Jack Keene had a thing for rocks. One Lexington horseman said of him that for every dollar he made, he spent fifty cents on stone.

Maybe that's why he went broke. From Keeneland's opening-day booklet: "All of this Mr. Keene had planned to bequeath to the citizens of Lexington. Reverses during the Depression, however, forced him to halt construction of his dream."

Work on the track at Keeneland Stud ground to a halt. Some projects—the stone-walled indoor training track for instance—would go unfinished. Jack Keene spent $400,000 on the track before he finally gave up.

Enter a group of men looking to develop a track to take the place of the old Kentucky Association, which had been falling apart. The city was squeezing the track in, and the physical plant was deteriorating. In 1933 the Kentucky Association ran its last meet.

Many Lexington horse folks were nostalgic about the K.A., but at the same time they were undoubtedly embarrassed by it. Much the way I feel about Aqueduct, I suppose. I love the place, but it's not where I go when someone says they would love to go to the track and learn something about horse racing. I wait until the spring and bring them out to Belmont. First impressions are important.

As early as 1920, a Colonel Bradley had threatened to organize a group to create a new racetrack. Although Keene was broke, his project doomed, he still dreamed of the place. So a bit of the Keene land would leave the family after all. He sold his track to Colonel Bradley and company. Keene had made a good start, after all, as such fixtures as the 500,000-gallon water tank would certainly convey. The track at Keeneland Stud looked as if another $300,000 was needed to complete it.

MIDWAY up the backstretch, Velasquez nudged Alydar. Velasquez didn't like how far out Raymond Earl was getting. Alydar was running wide and had been well held for a mile. Velasquez had rated him perfectly; there was a lot of gas in the tank. Alydar would go when asked.

At the half-mile, Velasquez decided to make his move.

"I moved a little earlier and a little stronger at the half-mile pole than I had planned to because I saw that horse on the lead was pretty far out there," Velasquez said later.

The Markeys were again making their way to the rail. They would be there when the field turned for home. Mrs.

Markey would wave a white-gloved hand in the air and cheer her baby on.

Alydar came barreling around the turn. He was fourth going into the turn. On the outside, he moved with a rush and took the lead. He had six lengths by the time he hit the stretch. The Markeys cheered for their beautiful chestnut with a star on his forehead, as his diagonal white socks snapped at the dirt. He was running away with it. The Calumet blood horse was the best horse in the country that day. Alydar was the real thing, and he was giving his owners a hell of a show.

Velasquez tapped Alydar two or three times to keep his mind on the race, and Alydar romped home thirteen and a half lengths ahead of Raymond Earl.

That Alydar had been the overwhelming favorite was clear—1-10 is pretty short. The odds on the place, show, and the fourth horse were 28, 52, and 60 to 1. No horse but Alydar was on the tote board, and at the wire it was still true. Keeneland had restricted the betting to just win and place, but still the crowd of 22,512 had laid so heavily on Alydar that both pools were negative. The win pool was $9,822.75 short, and there was a minus place pool of $25,253.70. All bets paid $2.20.

Raymond Earl had held by a nose for second over Go Forth. Sunny Songster was another two lengths back.

When the results were made official, the two country sophisticates at the rail on the turn hobbled toward each other. Mrs. Markey put her cheek to her husband's for a moment.

After Veitch and Velasquez received the Keeneland julep cup in the winner's circle from the governor of Kentucky, the whole group—the governor, the press, the jockey, the trainer—advanced to the station wagon. The governor handed the julep cup through the window to Mrs. Markey. The winner's circle had come to the Markeys. The trophy was handed into the car. They smiled. It was the last race either of them ever saw.

AT THE DERBY, Alydar was beaten by Affirmed, and their rivalry would become famous. It continued in the Preakness and ended in one of the most brilliant stretch duels of all time in the Belmont Stakes. In all three races, Affirmed was the victor. He won the last Triple Crown of the seventies, the most recent one as of this writing—twenty-six years ago, the longest stretch ever.

In Affirmed's first eighteen starts, he lost only to Alydar. The two horses raced ten times. Affirmed won seven.

In the Triple Crown duels, Affirmed had one and a half lengths at the Derby, a neck at the Preakness, and a head at the Belmont. In horse racing, a length is traditionally considered to equal a fifth of a second. Affirmed's margin of victory was just about two-fifths of a second over all three races. Over their ten races, they ran 10-5/16 miles. Affirmed's total margin of victory was about four and a half lengths. Over the ten miles they ran against each other, when the dust settled there was about a second separating the two.

Any other year would have belonged to Alydar. Even Laz Barra, Affirmed's trainer, felt that was the case. She added that Affirmed "needed a colt like Alydar to make him run."

In the Preakness it looked as if Affirmed might cave in when Alydar rushed up to him in the stretch. He cocked his right ear toward Alydar and held on.

Jorge Velasquez, Alydar's jockey, remarked, "Trying to pass Affirmed is like running into a wall."

Chick Lang, who was running Pimlico then, told the press: "I can hardly believe what I saw. Affirmed had his neck fully extended and his teeth bared, like a fighter closing in for the kill."

The 1978 Belmont Stakes was one of the best horse races ever run. Alydar ran a different type of race that day; he was up and challenging Affirmed as early as the clubhouse turn. By the time the horses got to the big sandy backstretch of Belmont, it was clear that the duel was between the two of them. They were opening up on the field, running against each other. The race had begun modestly, with a twenty-five-second quarter-mile. The two rivals had six lengths by the time they hit the stretch turn. They picked up the pace, neck and neck. Alydar poked a head in front on the stretch, but Steve Cauthen switched his whip hand and tapped Affirmed. Affirmed dug in and wouldn't give it up. The field might as well have been a mile up the track. There was just the two of them. When they hit the wire it was Affirmed by a nose.

Alydar became the only horse ever to be second in the Derby, the Preakness, and the Belmont Stakes.

LUCILLE MARKEY died July 24, 1982, having been royalty of the American turf for almost five decades. Gene Markey had gone in 1980. At Calumet, things slid.

Most of the Wright family didn't want much to do with horse racing. Mrs. Markey famously tried to keep the farm out of the control of her eldest son Warren, who didn't know a thing about horses. J. T. Lundy had married into the family. Lundy knew about horses, but that didn't help matters.

Lundy played very fast with Calumet, sinking it wildly into debt, creating businesses around the country, buying jets, and booking the stallions well into the future, thereby cashing checks now that wouldn't be earned for years.

On November 13, 1990, Alydar was found in his stall with a broken leg. The injury, suspicious to say the least, would kill him.

In 2000, Lundy went to jail. All of his dealings were suspect. For one thing, it's difficult to see where all the money went. Certainly there are a string of coincidences akin to the fact that the Lou-Roe stable in Ocala, Florida, run by a good friend of Lundy's and with which Calumet did a fair bit of business, was eventually seized and its owners indicted—the whole operation allegedly a money-laundering front for the Gambino crime family.

The connections may be oblique. I certainly don't know any more than Ann Auerbach, whose book *Wild Ride* documents the fall of Calumet. Even she was afraid to say anything too direct. To my eye, things like the Calumet relationship with Lou-Roe or Lundy's friendship with Robert Libutti (a high-stakes gambler, wild card, and reputed wiseguy) may not be unswervingly indicting but certainly set the tone for Lundy's tenure.

As the farm slid deeper into oblivion—ridiculously in debt, overbooked, poorly managed, overextended—a wave of lawsuits pushed Calumet over the brink. In the end, the Wright heirs were broke. One of them worked as a clerk in a Long John Silver's.

J. T. Lundy would have no such luck. In 2000 he was sentenced to four years for bank fraud. Many suspect he should be in jail for murdering Alydar. The horse had been insured for $36.5 million.

The farm would be rescued from oblivion by Henri de Kwiatkowski in 1992. He bought the whole place for seventeen million dollars. He couldn't let it die. Calumet, like Keeneland, had become a natural entity, a piece of Kentucky that seems to have been there forever and shouldn't be lost.

But before this, two icons of Kentucky horse country—Calumet and Keeneland—came together for a brilliant race in 1978. When Jack Keene started his fantasy track at Keeneland Stud, he said he wanted to see "Racing as it was meant to be." Keeneland picked up that motto. One spring day at the Blue Grass Stakes in 1978, it more than fulfilled its charter.

5
A Cool Million

Horse-racing Chicagoans have always seemed to me a forward-looking group. Arlington Park was modern from its inception. Conceived in 1926 to be built in the suburb of Chicago called Arlington Heights, the place showed none of the anxiety about history demonstrated so vividly at Keeneland. Perhaps the apprehensions that so clog the minds of the Kentucky hardboots don't bother folks in the Midwest. I suppose there are but few First Families of Virginia idly ruminating on their status on the shores of the Great Lake.

While Jack Keene hauled rock out of the ground and built Keeneland in accordance with ideas he'd picked up in England, as if it were in fact a kind of old country, H. D. Curley Brown envisioned a new park in Chicago welded together from steel and sheathed in glass. There would be no time wasted on a false sense of antiquity. There would be no nods to the Victorian betting parlor. Arlington Park didn't look like a horse farm. Corbusier could have built the old track at Arlington, so straight are the lines, so clear is the expression of function. The roof was one long plane, like a line out of Frank Lloyd Wright's Prairie Style. This was a modern sports venue, a twentieth-century grandstand, a celebration of entertainment. Thinking about this space in the context of Brownie Leach's words from that Keeneland bulletin—a place "where friends could gather and match their horses, free from undesirable phases of the sport"—makes the contrast salient. This place celebrated all phases of the sport.

Over the course of his career, Curley Brown developed racetracks in Havana, Montana, New Orleans, Maryland, and elsewhere. To a consortium of businessmen (Laurance Armour, John Hertz, Weymouth Kirkland, Otto Lehman, and Major Frederick Mclaughlin, owner of a hockey team) he pitched his big, modern, populist facility on a thousand acres outside of Chicago. It would seat eighteen thousand and stable more horses than any racing facility in the nation. It would have its own railway station, so folks from the city could get to it easily. The racetrack would be two ovals, dirt on the outside, turf on the inside.

It would be the turf that set the tone at Arlington: the oldest type of race at the newest type of track.

Most tracks today have a turf course inside the dirt track. These grass ovals are much harder to maintain, and races on them are limited. Just imagine a dozen horses running full blast across your lawn. It takes a crew, and it takes care.

In 1665, when the first race was run on Salisbury, Long Island, it was run on grass. When the Union Race Course stripped the oval and found that the dirt underneath made for faster running and less maintenance, it made such sense that by the time of the Civil War racing had all but abandoned the grass surface. A couple of grass courses could still be found at the turn of the century—one was built at Saratoga in 1902 but abandoned in 1905.

Turf racing was slightly more successful in Coney Island. The historian Alan Carter wrote: "In 1886, the Coney Island Jockey Club built a one-mile turf course within its Sheepshead Bay track, and on June 10 of that year Dry Monopole won the Green Grass Stakes on that new course. Turf racing continued to be popular at Sheepshead Bay until the track closed in 1910, when betting at New York race tracks was declared illegal."

In the early thirties, two new turf tracks were built, at Arlington and Hialeah, Florida. The races run on them were at first considered to be exhibition races, mere entertainments. But by the close of the decade, they had begun running for real money. Hialeah inaugurated the $5,000 Miami Beach Handicap.

The first turf race at Arlington was run in 1934. It was the first in Illinois. In 1941 the Arlington Handicap, an important race, was switched to grass. In 1942, demonstrating that it already considered turf to be an important part of its racing scene, Arlington became the first course in America to bank the turns on its turf course.

Advancement was the program at Arlington, whether it was in steel and glass, in the improvement and exploitation of the oldest racing surface available, or in the general elevation of the sport. Chicago racing had been a rough-and-tumble scene. Sportsman's Park, for instance, had been founded in the twenties by Al Capone as a dog track and converted to thoroughbred racing only after dog racing was declared illegal. Arlington was another world. It was clean (literally and figuratively), and had swimming pools, tennis courts, and polo fields. There were many racetracks in Chicago, but Arlington was premier from the start.

In other words, Curley Brown's plan bore fruit. Mostly, however, harvesting was done without Curley. His small consortium ran out of money almost immediately, and in 1929 the plant was sold to twenty businessmen who incorporated it as the Arlington Jockey Club. The history of ownership at Arlington Park has a lot to do with the spirit of its management and the way it has been run through the years. It would change hands again in 1940, purchased by John D. Allen (of Brinks & Company) and Ben Lindheimer, the director of Washington Park on Chicago's South Side. The two parks coordinated their racing schedules and together ran Chicago's racing season. Lindheimer ran Arlington for twenty years until his death from a heart attack in 1960. His daughter, Marje Everett, inherited control of the track.

Marje Everett can be a daunting character to this day, but when she worked at Arlington she was downright scary. "No comment," is the most frequent answer I've gotten when asking about working with her. Sometimes followed by something like "Ha ha, yeah . . . boy . . . she was tough." In *Classic* magazine, Whitney Tower quoted one director of Arlington Park (called just that, no name given) as having said: "If Marje Everett has one chief fault, it is a willingness not to listen to other people's advice." Another Arlington exec observed, "Her needs are simple. All she wants out of life is her own way about everything."

In 1967 the track was merged with Gulf and Western, and in 1971 it was bought by the Madison Square Garden Company. MSG owned it for the next dozen years, and presided over its most prosperous and outrageous invention: the Arlington Million.

No one had ever run a race for a million dollars. It was an amazing amount of money. And Arlington intended to run it on turf and to attract an international field. A million bucks, on the grass, in Chicago.

MSG had sent a vice president to run the track, a man from New York named Joe Joyce. The usual story goes that one day Joyce was absentmindedly gazing out his office window at the beautiful turf course, thinking that Arlington needed a major event, a real attraction, something splendid to put Arlington Park on the map and people in the seats. He came up with the idea of a million-dollar race.

Bill Thayer, senior vice president of racing at Arlington, says this common wisdom isn't really the way it happened. "Bullshit," he says.

Bill is one of the great figures of American racing. At seventy-eight he still goes in every day, as he has since the early 1970s. He more or less expects that when he leaves the track, it will be feet first. "It's the greatest game to get old in," Bill told me. "Everywhere I go, I know somebody." He misses a lot of his old friends—he used to eat dinner with famed jockey Bill Shoemaker once a week—"but there's new people too."

Joe Joyce bills himself as the father of the Arlington Million, and that upsets Bill. "Depends on the meaning of father, I guess. The million had a lot of midwives. I don't know who the father of the thing is." But he knows the story of how the race came to be.

A man named Earl Webster, who ran a shipping company called Thoroughbred International, and who later was a blood-stock agent, called Bill Thayer in 1970 or 1971. Earl had a big idea he wanted to talk about. They met for lunch. Bill took notes on his napkin.

"How'd you like to run a race for a million dollars?" asked Earl.

Bill thought he was nuts at first. "Where do we get that kind of money?"

"Sponsors. Advertising."

They hashed it out. Earl had imagined it would be a race for three-year-olds; Bill suggested they open it up, make it three-year-olds *and up.* That way it would attract more international horses. In Argentina the horses all turn one year old in the summer. In the United States they all turn one in January. If you want to get international horses involved, you've got to make the age restrictions translatable.

Bill took the idea to Jack Loome, Arlington's president. Loome asked if Bill had been drinking. In 1971 the Kentucky Derby was worth $145,500 to the winner, with a total purse of $183,000. A million dollars was an incredible amount of money for a single horse race.

Bill explained the race. A million dollars, the big time, an international field. Eventually he convinced Loome, and they took the idea to Madison Square Garden. Irving Felt, chairman of the board, said, "You guys find the money." That was the end of that.

But Bill kept the idea in his desk, and a few years later he tried again. Joe Joyce was now Arlington's president, and Joyce took the project to MSG again.

"Pretty good idea. You guys find the money."

That was the end of that.

In the early 1980s, Bill and Joe Joyce saw their chance. Sonny Werblin was chairing Madison Square Garden.

"Sonny was a showman," said Bill. "A promoter. He loved the big tent." Werblin had purchased the American Football League team called the Titans of New York and changed its name to the New York Jets. In 1965 he signed Joe Namath with a staggering bonus of $400,000. Quarterbacks made about a tenth of that at the time.

Namath was immediately a long-haired superstar, flaunting his new wealth by wearing a full-length fur coat on the sidelines. In 1968 he led the Jets against the Baltimore Colts in the third Super Bowl. Hall of Fame quarterback Norm Van Brocklin, deprecating the American Football League, remarked, "This will be Namath's first professional football game." The Jets won.

Sonny Werblin was a man who understood the value of throwing money around, and he understood how to gamble. His gamble on the Titans and the young Joe Namath had paid off big time.

The MSG people asked longtime turf writer Joe Hirsch what he thought, and he said it was a good idea. Hirsch asked some trainers in England if they'd come, and they said yes.

Says Bill: "So, Sonny said 'Let's go.' I don't know who the father of the million is, I don't know what the definition of 'father' is. Why don't you look it up for me?"

In December 1980, 1,287 horses were nominated to the race, and their owners put up $1,000 each for the possibility of entering the race. On June 1, 87 were kept eligible, and they kicked in second-round stakes money of $2,500 each. On July 30 the third-round fees came due, and 52 entries coughed up $3,500 each. Fourteen starters and 10 alternates were chosen from that field.

Steven Crist, turf writer at the *New York Times* in the early eighties (he went on to become publisher of the *Daily Racing Form* and author of *Betting on Myself*), was skeptical. "It's a bust," one official of the New York Racing Association told him. "International racing just is not something that can ever capture American fan interest. You can't expect bettors to get excited about horses they've never heard of and can't get a line on."

Crist wrote that "the ambitious goal to make the race an instant classic and its promoters' insistence on exaggerating what otherwise would be considered a successful first effort have put the race on trial. The track's ongoing hyperbole has antagonized some segments of the industry and encouraged skepticism from the public and the press. Arlington does itself little good by advertising the 14 who will go to the post today as the 'Finest Field in Thoroughbred History,' because a long string of defections eliminated almost half the original field and many other top runners were not nominated." Crist pointed out that "the track had to go all the way down to the

10th alternate—Match the Hatch—to fill the 14 positions in the starting gate. Six of the top 14 choices, all near the top of anyone's ranking of the field, were among the defections, including the sole representatives of four foreign countries."

But Arlington had its horses. By post time there would be only twelve in the gate, but the dozen would run a race for a million dollars, and they would run it over the Chicago turf.

So a few of the dozen were alternates, and the field in Chicago wasn't exactly the international collection of champions for which Arlington had hoped. Still, some very heavy hitters were among the horses being called to the post.

Among them was the six-year-old gelding John Henry. Red Smith wrote that John Henry had been born on the wrong side of the tracks, "so far over on the wrong side that he couldn't hear the train whistle."

He was of ridiculous conformation, modest pedigree, and horrible disposition. No one is going to the auction looking for a badly put together, poorly blooded, nasty youngster.

John Henry was calf-kneed, a condition generally considered serious, which greatly increases the likelihood of injury. If one views a well-conformed horse from the side, the hind leg structure will have a plum line from the point of the buttocks to the ground. The line should touch the hocks, run parallel to the cannon, and be slightly behind the heel. The front leg of a perfectly conformed horse will have a similar plum line that drops from the first joint of the shoulder, right through the second, then touches the front of the knee, and lands at the top of the hoof right where it begins, bisecting that hoof. On a calf-kneed horse, the front knees are set behind or back in the horse's leg, as if curling under. The next joint, which on ourselves we would call the calf or shin, seems to bow out backward. Calf knees allow the knees to bend backward, and calf-kneed horses tend to get hurt.

John Henry's sire, Old Bob Bowers, had managed to pay for his feed by getting up into the money in a couple of minor stakes races, but overall he went to the post a lot more than he went to the winner's circle. The dam, Once a Double, had earned $3,123 over the course of her illustrious career. Back up the family tree, we find Bull Lea, Princequillo, Mahmoud, and some of the big names of the game, but they seem a long way from John Henry.

To make matters worse, he was and is an absolute schmuck of a horse. He now lives across the hall from Cigar at the Kentucky Horse Park, and when I met him he tried to bite his handler, my wife, an old fellow in a wheelchair, and me. At his first auction, when he was a yearling, he managed to jump around in his stall enough to smash his head in to something. When he took to the ring, where a horse should gleam like a new watch, he had blood running down his head. When the gavel came down, a mere $1,100 was lighting the board.

John Henry would rip his feed tubs off the wall, kick, and bite you. That's how he got his name. He ripped a tub off the wall, stomped on it, picked it back up in his teeth, and threw it into a gathering of people. One of his caretakers laughed and said, "Now there's a steel-driving horse." It stuck.

In 1977 he was back in the auction ring, where Harold Snowden, Jr., of Lexington picked him up for $2,200. Snowden liked him on the track but was annoyed by his temperament.

His pedigree wasn't about to send him off on a good stud career, so he was gelded.

Although gelding a horse usually is followed by a great improvement in disposition, John Henry stayed sour. Snowden sold him for $10,000 to Louisiana owners. He won a race, they bumped him up, and he won a stakes at the old Evangeline Downs in Louisiana. Then he lost nine in a row and went back to Snowden in a trade for two younger horses. Eventually he wound up in Sam Rubin's hands. Rubin's trainer Bob Donato began running him on grass, and he started winning. He went out nineteen times and won six. By the end of the year he'd picked up $120,000 and won a stakes race. The next year, when Donato stopped training for Rubin, John Henry was shipped out to California and Ron McAnally. They fit like custom-made shoes. John Henry won six in a row.

As a five-year-old, John Henry was no happier, but he was even faster. He started twelve times, won eight, and was never out of the money. He won $925,217 that year.

This was the John Henry that arrived in Arlington Park in the summer of 1981. He was six, and at the top of the game. The $1,100 yearling had earned more than a million dollars. Going into the Million, he'd run thirty-two races on grass and had been out of the money only twice.

He was far from alone, however.

A serious horse named Argument had arrived from France, with an American stakes victory at Laurel under his belt. From England came Madam Gay, who had placed in the Epsom and Irish derbies and had run well in a couple of stakes races across the pond. Leading Brit jock Lester Piggott was up on Madam

Gay, having made the trip for a shot at the million. Ireland sent Fingal's Cave. Paul Mellon's Rokeby Stable sent Key to Content, a four-year-old son who seemed to be running at top form. From Canada came Ben Fab. A five-year-old named Rossi Gold walked from the Spendthrift stables at Arlington to the track over which he trained. He had won four races over that grass and was a local favorite. Wrote Red Smith at the time: "Ladbroke's of London issued its first betting line on the Arlington Million and made Rossi Gold 20-1. The overseas switchboard lit up like a Christmas tree as horse players rang long distance."

The rest of the field was basically ignored, including a California horse called The Bart, who would go off at 40-1.

John Henry, in slot number five, was even money.

Key to Content jumped out front. He was running slow, posting fractions that weren't threatening even over the soft turf. But the pressure was on him from the start. The longshot California horse was breathing down his neck right away. The Bart didn't let him have any more than half a length lead throughout the race. He was relentless. Eddie Delahoussaye kept him right up there, pushing Key to Content, not giving him an inch. They were by themselves most of the way, with a length and a half between them and the field at the half-mile. At the mile they were two and a half lengths out. The Bart was tightening the screws. Key to Content had only a head in front.

Most of the field was turning in a pretty sad show. Regarding the back of the pack, the official chart says that Mrs. Penny "was outrun early, passed tiring rivals." Indeed, the horse was twelfth for most of the race and drifted forward to seventh by the wire. Rossi Gold started out just ahead of Mrs. Penny, in eleventh, "was not asked for early speed, swung wide after seven furlongs, but failed to respond in drive." Super Moment got himself up in the race to start, but "gradually gave way between horses." Kilijaro was through after five furlongs. Fingal's Cave showed little. P'tite Tete was "forwardly placed early outside horses faltered nearing second turn."

All of which is to say that John Henry had some traffic to get through.

John Henry was off slow. Willie Shoemaker was in no rush to get him up in the race. He lost ground going around the first turn, but by the time they came out of it he was well settled on the inside, running comfortably in eighth. It was the plan to keep him off the pace, but not this far back. "I was looking at some charts of Arlington turf races earlier today," John Henry's trainer Ron McAnally told the press after the race. "I noticed that very few horses win on the lead here, so I told Shoemaker to take him back a little. But I didn't expect to see him that far out."

"I was wide at the beginning and had to drop in to the inside," said Shoemaker. "I knew I had enough horse—I just hoped I had enough ground."

Before he could even worry about the ground, Shoemaker was forced to avoid all these buckling horses down the backstretch. The whole run down the far side of the track had a kind of backward drift to it, as horses dropped like flies, wilt-

ing in front of John Henry and the Shoe. And he had to somehow get around them all and preserve his horse.

Shoemaker was fifty, he'd won more than eight thousand
races, and still he was surprised. "I was kind of fooled by the
way the race was run. I thought we'd have a easy time getting
out, but the others fooled me."

It was a masterful ride to get John Henry through the traffic at all. But he was doing it. All along the backstretch, John
Henry improved his position.

Up front, The Bart was still pressuring Key to Content,
breathing down his neck. It was a slow pace, but there was no
mercy, no room to wiggle up there in front of the field.

Eddie D. spurred The Bart in the turn.

John Henry was weaving his way to the front behind him.
Ticking off the horses, one after the other. Eddie D. wasn't
worried about him yet. Key to Content was digging in; he
wouldn't give up without a fight. Finally, after battling around
the turn, Key to Content caved in coming into the stretch, and
The Bart took the lead.

On the stretch, John Henry made his way past all the other
horses and found another gear. When he straightened out and
the Shoe said "Go!" he rolled like a boulder down the stretch.
But the Bart had momentum too. He wasn't about to let John
Henry swish on by him. Eddie D. had his whip in his right
hand, and he was imploring The Bart to dig down deep. The
Bart kept on.

John Henry surged up behind him, and for the final yards
the two horses were rivals, dead against each other, neither

taking the lead by more than a breath. The Shoe was driving John Henry hard. Eddie D. was tucked up on The Bart, very forward, begging him.

This is why you come to the races, and the crowd loved it. The 40-1 shot and the even-money favorite hit the wire together.

Bill Thayer was in a box in front of John Sullivan, who trained The Bart. He turned and said, "John, go get your picture taken."

"I was hoping I had won, but it was too close to tell," Delahoussaye said. "I told Shoemaker, 'I think you beat me,' and he said, 'I'm not sure.'"

The richest thoroughbred race ever run was looking like a dead heat. For six worrying minutes, the photo sign flashed on the tote board. Steve Crist wrote, "Sam Rubin, the New York bicycle importer who bought John Henry three years ago for $25,000, stared at the tote board for the six minutes after the 'photo-finish' sign stayed up."

John Henry's number came up.

Crist: "Rubin jumped a foot off the ground and yelled, 'I knew it! I was saying to myself all this time, "I know we got him, I know we got him," and we did!'"

A lot of horsemen, and even more fans, believe that horses know it when they win. They seem to walk to the winner's circle with little jaunty steps, ears pricked. They seem proud. I suppose if this were the wild, they'd have just proved that the herd of fillies was rightfully their own. Perhaps they are a little cocksure, but John Henry demonstrated no such thing. He was exhausted. Arlington wanted a lengthy presentation,

Willie Shoemaker (foreground) wins the first Arlington Million on John Henry.

crowding as many people as possible into the winner's circle. John Henry was not in the mood. He refused to be controlled. He spun and wheeled about, snorting. He kicked mud on anyone near him. They let him go back to the stall. I'm sure he tried to bite his groom on the way, and ripped his water bucket off the wall when he got there. God knows how they got a urine sample from him to test it for dope.

Although attendance at the first Arlington Million was about ten thousand shy of the estimates—and hopes—of the Arlington management, the race was an instant classic. This was due in no small part to the fact that it had been so dramatically decided. John Henry and the Million were immediately linked. He returned for the third Million in 1983, and again he fought it out on the stretch. Chris McCarron was up in the irons now, and kept John Henry up on the pace with Nijinky's Secret. But the British import Tolomeo got past him on the stretch and won. Incredibly, John Henry later returned as a nine-year-old. (Since they have no stud prospects, geldings tend to hang around the racetrack for a while.) A record crowd of 39,053 came out to Arlington and bet John Henry down to the favorite. Chris McCarron again got him up in the race, but this time they blew by the pace-setting Royal Heroine and coasted to a one-and-three-quarters-length victory.

That purse pushed John Henry over the $5 million mark, the first horse to reach that figure. In 1984 he was named Horse of the Year.

The next year would bring a test of spirit the likes of which Arlington couldn't imagine. The fifth Arlington Million was a long shot, a 100-1 dark horse. It shouldn't have been possible.

Wednesday, July 31, 1985, a small fire started in the Post and Paddock Club, a building of white with blue awnings that sat to the west of Curley Brown's big grandstand. The fire was discovered at 1:30 A.M., and the alarm went up at the Arlington Heights fire department at 2:15. The fire spread and raged through the night, battled by 150 firefighters summoned from 25 communities. Racetrackers, backside staff, firemen, police, and the administration battled the blaze. They fought to little or no avail. The firestorm raged. The place went up like a tinderbox—all was lost, the entire track reduced to rubble.

Bill Thayer was on hand that night, and he almost got himself arrested when he ran into the offices to get the foal papers. He figured that without them, racing in Illinois would be

Twisted girders were about all that remained after the 1985 fire at Arlington.

as good as done. Most folks figured Arlington was done for, with or without the equine records that Bill saved.

But in 1983, two years after the first Million, a small group had purchased Arlington. Among them was a man named Dick Duchossois.

Duchossois had made a fortune in railroads and hadn't expected to get caught up in racing. He started in a small way, owning a couple of horses, going to the Derby, but it became more and more a part of his life. A couple of weeks before the fire, he had quit his other businesses to work at the track full time.

Duchossois has been a controversial figure in Chicago racing. Most of the people who work with and for Mr. D. adore him. He is capable of dramatic gestures and seems to carry on Arlington's forward-looking, risk-taking, gutsy traditions.

Others believe he is little more than a greedy, flashy, megalomaniac businessman. In a dispute over gambling legislation, he closed the track in the late nineties and let it stand shuttered for two seasons. Duchossois told King Kaufman of *Salon*: "You have to bear in mind, this is agribusiness. The racetrack is just the tip of the iceberg out here. You've got the farmer, the breeder, the guy that grows the wheat, the hay, the oats, the guy that drives the trucks, the veterinarian, the veterinarian schools, all these other things that come on up. I would say for every man at the race track, you probably have eight to ten people back on the farm supporting that horse."

Which is exactly why many took such offense at his closing down Arlington, feeling that he was taking the dispute out on the wrong people.

Duchossois displayed exactly the opposite spirit that wretched summer of 1985. First, amid the charred ashes, seeing his colleagues and employees in tears as the fire was struck, he walked around telling them not to worry. "We'll be back." He told Bill Thayer it was a "blessing in disguise, better to go now."

Duchossois picked up the bill at the track kitchen, feeding the staff for free while they shipped horses to Hawthorne for racing.

In twenty-five days at Arlington, workers managed to clear enough rubble and erect enough tents to stage the 1985 Million, which won them an Eclipse Award of Merit. That race is now known as the Miracle Million.

In 1986, Duchossois bought out the other shareholders and took sole control of Arlington. He flew around the world investigating tracks, looking for ideas for his new, modern racing facility. He was determined that the best track in the world would rise from the ashes. Did he succeed? It's an impossible distinction to make, but I've heard many persons say that Arlington is their favorite place. When the track reopened in 1987, racing fans were in for a treat. The new Arlington International Racecourse is sparkling white, with great curves of glass and a dramatic cantilevered roof. The grounds are fastidiously gardened. Hall of Fame trainer D. Wayne Lukas has said that if you wanted to introduce someone to horse racing, this would be the place to do it. Because the roof is cantilevered, there are no pillars, and every seat in the house has an unimpaired view. The floors shine. The bathrooms are sparkling clean. The betting area behind the box seats is one of the most gracious places I've ever gambled—long curved tables of richly stained wood, soft lighting, and smiling help. It's a knockout.

King Kaufman collected a few opinions about the place in his article about the 2002 Breeders' Cup. "As far as the aesthetic beauty of a racetrack, as far as the modern-day racetrack, it's second to none," says Chris McCarron, the Hall of Fame jockey who retired this summer. "Other racetracks have a lot of historical mystique and charm. This track falls more into the category of your modern stadium." Dr. John Chandler, president of Juddmonte Farms, says, "We'd rather win here than anyplace else."

Today, like always, Arlington is a unique place. It has not rested on its traditions or allowed itself to fade. On Friday night the place is packed for happy hour. On a Saturday afternoon the beautiful landscaping is in bloom and the curved glass and brilliant white of the grandstand all shine. This ain't your grandfather's track, I'm telling you.

6
Pack Up Your Bit and Git

I lived in California briefly as a child, but I hadn't been back since. I hadn't been west of Chicago in twenty-five years. I had smugly satisfied myself that the Left Coast was uninteresting, that the Eastern seaboard was where it was at—a clichéd sensibility, I'm aware. New Yorkers "know" that LA is a vapid, plastic place filled with money-hungry movie people and dumb blondes. Somehow it never occurs to us that NYC is a vapid, concrete place filled with money-hungry financial people and exhausted brunettes. As I flew over an increasingly foreign landscape of seemingly endless khaki deserts and sharp-edged mountains, I began to feel energized. Even from the little portal window of my plane I began to formulate a new impression of the West. It was different. It was divorced from any hangups about heritage or history. It was utterly American, free-wheeling, dusty, and maverick. Driving up La Brea from LAX on my way to the Hollywood Hills where I was lucky enough to be staying with an old friend of the family (and such a track bum that he has degenerated into playing the biggest gamble of all: actually owning thoroughbreds), I took to the light of the place immediately. I liked the gritty MexiCali feel of the landscape. A roadside restaurant sold both tacos and pastrami—just move me in across the street. I crested a hill and saw another hill in front of me dotted with citrus trees and cute little bungalow houses, and I snapped. I'd been ripped off. I'd been conned. Some publicity group for grim Eastern cities had put bum information in my head. Los Angeles is beautiful. Who knew?

It turned out that a lot of people knew that Los Angeles was beautiful, and those who did not could not be convinced. I made phone calls back east from a patio that overlooked the huge bowl of Los Angeles. I stared at that funky old pile of 45s that is the Capitol Record building. "Yeah, well, I'm not coming back. I'm moving here," I teased, which was untrue but gives a sense of my enthusiasm for the place.

And I hadn't even seen Santa Anita.

Driving out to Arcadia, you see the big mountains and the lush grass and everything is green and palmy and breezy and wonderful.

The confluence of California influences at Santa Anita is astonishing. On the backside it can feel like a dude ranch. Spanglish fills the air, and the breeze is redolent with hay and horse sweat. Pepper trees line the dirt avenues. The barns and stables are low, ranch style.

The grandstand itself is like a deco palace, a giant train. Relief figures of racing thoroughbreds adorn the windows. The railings on the balconies are sculpted palm-tree arabesques painted desert yellow. Kumquats grow around the paddock, and they're delicious.

Then there's the deluxe turf club, with its chandeliers and potted palms. Soft chairs are arranged perfectly around the room, as if waiting for the swish of silk and the thin curl of cigarette smoke, as if it was built to host a Cary Grant and Ingrid Bergman kiss.

The mountains loom always. In fog the San Gabriel Mountains can look serene, like a Japanese landscape painting. In the sunlight they change character entirely and look like a dusty scrub-brush backdrop for a Western movie, somewhere you'd hide out from the posse, or something you'd have to cross in a covered wagon.

One should see all racetracks in the early morning, but nowhere is this more true than at Santa Anita. It's an intimate and friendly time. The little spot down by the stretch turn, which they call Clocker's Corner, has been operating for years. Trainers, jockey agents, hacks, fans, and the eponymous clockers all mingle over steaming coffee as the horses walk by, nervous and eager to get to the exercise. Horses want to run.

I sat with a plate of chorizo and eggs staring at the beautiful mountains, and the beautiful horses, and listening to the exercise riders cluck at their high-strung mounts. *Hup hup hup hup comeoncomeoncomeon migo, migo, cluck cluck cluck cálmate, cálmate, okay, okay big fella,* stopping the chatter only long enough to say hello to someone leaning on the rail, or joke with another rider. The dry California air of Arcadia was crystal clear. The Stute brothers were sitting at the next table with their own breakfasts and their crisp Stetson hats. They had been at Santa Anita since opening day 1934 and were still training there. The outriders were riding painted ponies and wearing cowboy hats. The dirt on the track was dark. Down in Clocker's Corner, you're right at face level with the track. The horses come pounding around the turn, snorting a shot of breath with each step, and they seem so close.

ELIAS JACKSON BALDWIN, AKA "Lucky," was a grocery-store owner, saloonkeeper, and hotelier in Indiana and Wisconsin who traveled west by wagon train in 1853, following the prospectors. Too sharp to wildcat, he made his money selling provisions, liquor, and hotel rooms in San Francisco and dived into the sizzling real estate market there.

When prospectors began to look elsewhere, San Francisco began to cool. Gold had been discovered by a Californian in Australia, and in 1858 prospectors also began migrating in huge numbers to Canada and Colorado, chasing gold.

Then came the big hit, the mother, perhaps the biggest single mineral strike ever discovered: the Comstock Lode. Thousands poured into Nevada to make their fortunes. Towns sprung up overnight. Fortunes were made quickly and lost bitterly. Comstock would have long-term repercussions not just for Baldwin but for all of America. Comstock would be the foundation of the Hearst millions. Mark Twain failed at prospecting there and found himself working for the local newspaper in the mining town of Virginia City, where a commodities market developed. Still too cautious or shrewd to prospect himself, Baldwin threw himself into the market and played all out. He was becoming rich—rich enough to begin thinking about a Grand Tour.

In 1867, Lucky Baldwin packed up his clothes, the key to the safe, and, I would imagine from the pictures I've seen of him, a deck of cards, and lit out to see the world. He left his broker a sell order—if his shares of silver fell too far, get out.

He hunted elephants in India and sailed to Japan. He picked up some Japanese entertainers and took them back to New York, where he turned a stint as a vaudeville producer. When he got back to San Francisco, he was in for some news.

His shares of silver stock had fallen far below his sell order, but his broker was unable to get out of the market because the certificates were in the safe, and the key to the safe was in Lucky's pocket. Here's where Lucky earned his name: since Lucky had been gone so long, the stock had come out of its slump and soared to new, unimagined heights. He had made millions of dollars.

Now wildly loaded, he went south to fulfill his dream, which seems to have been twofold. One: ditch the wife and set out on a long-term project of philandering. Two: buy some good thoroughbreds and become a breeder.

He bought 63,000 acres in the shadow of the San Gabriel Mountains, and named the farm Santa Anita Rancho. He spent sacks of money on good Kentucky horses, including the great Calfornia sire Emperor of Norfolk. He was a fast son of Norfolk, and under Lucky's silks he won twenty-one of twenty-nine starts.

Mary Fleming recorded the end of Emperor of Norfolk's racing career in her book *The History of the Throughbred in California.*

> Emperor of Norfolk was ruined because of a senseless wager at Washington Park. The world record for a mile was then 1:39-3/4, a record which had not been approached for years. At the time, Emperor of Norfolk was rounding into his finest form and had never been better. One morning, his regular exercise rider casually bet a friend that the Emperor could not only tie the mile record, but lower it as well. With several watches on him, the strapping bay colt proceeded to do just that. He traveled the distance in 1:38, unofficially slashing nearly two seconds off of Ten Broeck's long-standing record.

But the effort had destroyed him. His tendons were in ruin. (One can only imagine what happened to that rider.) Emperor of Norfolk was shipped back to Rancho Santa Anita, and Lucky hit the jackpot once again. As talented as he was on the track, the horse proved even more successful at stud.

Baldwin rolled along. His life was a torrent of women, horses, and poker games. He was in court so many times, defending himself against the accusations of women, that he is reported to have said in his defense that any woman who came anywhere near him must have known what they were in for, so public was his reputation.

He subdivided land and created the towns of Arcadia and Monrovia. A jilted lover shot him in the arm. A religious zealot took a shot at him in court and just missed his head.

In his old age he turned his attention to what is, at least in these pages, a familiar fantasy for the rich: he wanted to build the best racetrack anyone had ever seen. He built it on his ranch, and in December 1907, Lucky's Santa Anita held its first meeting. He addressed the crowd: "I desire no other monument. This is the greatest thing I have ever done, and I am satisfied." Racing lasted for 107 days, and the track was hailed as the most modern, most lavish facility in the West.

Baldwin died in 1909.

His Santa Anita racetrack would survive him by one year, until it was closed by the same nationwide anti-gambling movement that closed all the New York tracks in 1910. Tracks on the East Coast were running again by 1913, but the legislation out west stuck. There was no racing in California of any real consequence for two decades. Some exhibitions, some racing at fairs, but nothing real.

After some false starts, Hal Roach and Charles Strub teamed to reinvigorate the scene, and built a new track just a short distance from Lucky's original Santa Anita. Opening day was December 25, 1934.

Hal Roach had begun his working life as a prospector but quickly got into the movie business. Charles Strub was a San Francisco dentist and owner of a baseball team, who had been tying to develop a track in San Francisco. The partnership of Roach and Strub proved to be golden. The two sold shares door to door for five thousand dollars each, won all the approvals they needed, and started building 215 acres of Rancho Santa Anita they had purchased from Lucky's daughter Anita.

Seabiscuit wins the 1940 Santa Anita Handicap.

The new Santa Anita would jump-start the modern era of California racing. The owners thought big right out of the gate, offering a $100,000 purse in the Santa Anita Handicap, more money than had ever been offered for a single race.

IN 1966 a fifty-nine-year-old jockey announced that he was going to retire. His name was Johnny Longden, and he'd been racing in California since Seabiscuit was the star. Longden first hit the California circuit in 1930, thirty-six years earlier. He'd entered the Santa Anita winner's circle for the first time in 1936, aboard War Letter. Jim Murray wrote in the *Los Angeles Times* that racing without him would be "Unthinkable! Insupportable! France without love. Paris without spring. Italy without music. Germany without bands. Baseball without beer. Weddings without tears."

But it was true; Longden was done. He'd won more races than any other rider in history, 6,031, and the 1966 San Juan Capistrano at Santa Anita would be his last.

Worse yet, the Pumper, as Longden was known, was given but small chance to win his last outing. His mount, the Canadian-bred George Royal, had seen better days.

Don Richardson trained George Royal, and the horse had been good. He'd been a promising Canadian two-year-old, and at three he'd won nine consecutive races. As a four-year-old in 1965 he'd won this very race and had been Horse of the Year in Canada. But in 1966 he wasn't doing so well. He'd won a turf sprint in early January. After that he had begun to fade. He was out of the money in four starts. In his last outing before the San Juan Capistrano, he went off at long odds and finished pretty far up the track.

It didn't look like the fifty-nine-year-old jockey would go out in a blaze of glory. Nonetheless the mood was celebratory, regardless of Longden's chances. Jack Tobin wrote about the scene in *Sports Illustrated*. Willie Shoemaker denied that he wrote a sign posted in the jock's room: "John, Only 969 more to 7000. Sure you want to quit?—Shoe."

Longden was at the track all that day, from early morning, making rounds, talking to hot walkers and grooms, and hanging around the barns.

Lots of punters would push sentimental bets through the window that day, but even the love swelling in the chests of the sixty thousand in attendance could get the final odds down only to 6-1.

In the paddock, fans were calling out to Longden. "This is it, John!" "Go get 'em." Longden acknowledged his fans with a smile and a quick flip of his stick. Someone hollered, "Bring him in, John. Win one more." This was met with a wave of applause.

"Riders up!" was called in the paddock. Longden looked at his wife and friends.

Longden stepped into Richardson's hands—his last leg up. He'd ridden 32,479 races. He had one more to go.

"This is it," he said.

He spurred George Royal through the tunnel to the track.

Jack Tobin heard a fan ask, "'Is he going to try?' 'Man,' shot back a friend looking intently at the gnomelike jockey, 'he's all try.'"

When they broke out of the shade of the tunnel and into the smoggy grey light of the day, the crowd sent up a roar.

RIDING HORSES is not a job for fifty-nine-year-old men. A jock's life is a rough routine of sweatboxes, starvation diets, and flipping (as jocks jokingly refer to their career-specific version of bulimia). Jocks live in a weird dream world, required to control huge animals in dangerous situations at high speed while in a weakened state. They've been known to eat tapeworms. It's my understanding that they have, demographically speaking, a pretty high predilection for recreative drugs. There are few guarantees in their business, and they are victims of the whims of their owners and trainers. Only a small percentage of them actually make a substantial amount of money. If you don't win, and you don't get big rides or a long-term relationship with a stable, you end up piecing together a living fifty dollars at a time. William Murray observed that jockeys have the only job in the world where one is followed by an ambulance while at work.

Still, it's thrilling, and jockeys tend to love it. Gyle Konotopetz interviewed Longden for the *Calgary Herald* in 1993 and asked if he had any regrets.

"Did you ever work in a coal mine?" Longden replied.

Longden had. John Eric Longden was born in Wakefield, Lancashire, England, on Valentine's Day in 1907. His father and two of his brothers soon moved to Alberta, Canada, where there was work in the coal mines, leaving Johnny, his mother, and his three sisters behind until there was money enough to send for them. In 1912 the family was headed toward its reunion. Johnny, his sisters, and their mother would depart from Southampton in April. Their train was late. I don't know if that was Longden's first real stroke of luck, but it was certainly a good break. They'd bought passage on the *Titanic*, and they had to catch the next boat instead.

As a child, Longden worked the mule carts in the mines and went to school in Alberta. Another terrific California jockey named George Woolf (recently played by jockey Gary Stevens in the movie *Seabiscuit)* was a classmate. Woolf was known as "The Iceman" and was a great rider. He died at age thirty-six when he fell off his horse and hit his head on the rail.

While Longden was still a kid, a Native American taught him to ride horses "Roman style," straddling two horses bareback and riding them together. "After I learned that," Longden said, "getting on just one horse was easy."

He once quipped that he had gotten into racing because it seemed easier than mining coal.

In his teens, Longden moved to Calgary to work the counter at a cigar store called the Live Wire. Live Wire might seem a funny name for a cigar shop, but the shop was more of a betting parlor than a tobacconist. They made book in the back, and local racetrackers came around. Longden had to stand on an apple crate to reach the till. A trainer noticed him and bought him riding boots.

He began riding in the bush leagues, around the bullrings at the rough-riding Western tracks of Canada and the United States. In 1927 he hopped a freight train to Salt Lake City. On October 4, with borrowed tack and probably in his street clothes, he pushed a nine-year-old gelding, Hugo K. Asher, around the track and got him home in front to pay 16-1. It was Longden's first recorded victory; the horse never won again.

By 1930 he was traveling the circuit, running in British Columbia for the summer, where he was the leading rider that year, and in Cuba for winter racing, where he was the second-winningest jock.

Sunny Jim Fitzsimmons gave Longden his big break when he saw him up in the irons in Texas, and hired him to ride for the Phipps family's Wheatley Stable. In 1935, Longden rode Rushaway to two derby victories in two days, winning the May 22 Illinois Derby and the May 23 Latonia Derby. He was on a roll. Longden's streak would last for years, during which time he would notch the most important victories a man can win in this game, including the Triple Crown.

WHO KNOWS what went through Longden's mind as he steered a slightly faded George Royal up the hill to the gate at Santa Anita. The San Juan Capistrano is the funkiest race run in America. To lengthen the turf course, Santa Anita has a long spur that juts off the oval called the El Camino Real course. The horses run downhill on this chute and have to make a right turn, the only one at a thoroughbred track in America. The field is out of sight for a moment. Then they have to run across the dirt track before they hit the turf oval. Every time there's a big stakes race run down this crazy chute, a handful of articles are written about how the horses might freak out as they hit the dirt. Then another batch of articles comes along saying that the horses don't really care. Both sides have their evidence and supporters. It's always seemed to me that the jump across the dirt might perfectly well freak out both horse *and* rider, and would at the very least provide yet another excuse for losing.

THE BACKDROP for the Camino Real is the Los Angeles Arboretum, where the TV show "Fantasy Island" used to be filmed. It was part of Lucky Baldwin's original Santa Anita Rancho, and his peafowl still have the run of the place.

The peafowl are loud, and Longden must have heard them squawking as he rocked in the saddle.

LONDGEN was called the Pumper for his astonishing ability to get a horse out of the gate in front of the pack. But George Royal was not quick. This was made all the more clear when they broke from the gate. A horse named Plaque broke well and quickly, Bobby Ussery taking him to a good lead and pushing him down the hill. He was running alone, without pressure. The chart goes so far as to say that he was loafing, but Bill Hartack got Polar Sea hustling and joined the running out front. Once Hartack got Polar Sea up in the race, they began to force the pace. It had started as an easy time for Plaque, but he wasn't allowed to loiter for long.

Hill Rise, an excellent horse and the favorite, was slower, as was the Shoe's horse, Cedar Key. But none of them began the race with the languor that George Royal brought to the task. As the field charged down the crazy hill, George Royal raced by himself. Longden and his mount took the only right turn in America with ease, unhurried, and trotted down the Camino Real course as if it were a run in the park.

COUNT FLEET, he had been quick. Longden had met the brown colt as a gangly and bad-tempered youngster in John D. Hertz's barn. The colt was the son of Reigh Count, a racehorse Hertz had bought after watching him attempt to gain an advantage in a stretch duel by reaching out and biting a challenger. Reigh Count won the Kentucky Derby the following year.

Hertz bred him to speedy mares, hoping for a classic winner. He didn't know it, but this awkward and mean brown colt was the one he'd been looking for.

Longden knew it.

John D. Hertz was trying to sell him. He'd tried when the horse was a yearling and had gotten no takers. Now he was looking again; the asking price was $4,500.

"Don't do it," said Longden. "This horse loves to run."

"This colt's going to hurt somebody," Hertz said. "He's dangerous."

"He doesn't scare me," Longden said. "I'll win a lot of races with him."

Hertz kept Count Fleet, and Longden made good on his promise. He won a lot of races on him.

After his first couple of races as a two-year-old, the light went on. Count Fleet never finished out of the money, and he won ten of his last thirteen races in 1942. In the end-of-the-year Experimental Free Handicap he carried the ridiculous weight of 132 pounds (the highest weight ever assigned in that race's history).

This was just a preview of coming attractions. In 1943, Count Fleet was unstoppable. On April 13 that year he won an allowance race at Jamaica racetrack. Called to the post again four days later, he ran away with the Wood Memorial Stakes, winning by three and a half lengths. In the Kentucky Derby he faced nine three-year-olds, but it barely seemed like it. Count Fleet was the overwhelming favorite, and Longden got him out of the gate fast. He held his lead, cantered in front of the pack, and came home three lengths out front. A week later the Count did it again in Baltimore at the Preakness, but this time he drew off on the stretch and opened up eight lengths of daylight. Only three thoroughbreds had bothered to make the trip, and

Count Fleet toyed with them. Two weeks later he played with another short field to take the Withers Stakes. Again there were only three horses there to take him on, and none of them got anywhere near him.

At Belmont on June 5, 1943, the serious horses didn't even bother showing up. Two plodders were entered, Fairy Manhurst and Deseronto. They were a couple of solid allowance runners, and they may be the most nondescript pair of workhorses ever to duel for second place at the Belmont Stakes. They hooked up and fought it out until Fairy Manhurst finally shook Deseronto on the stretch and surged home to grab the place money by three-quarters of a length. The race had been won a full second earlier, when Count Fleet, kicking up a cloud of dust that on the old newsreel makes him look like a frenetic freight train, had bounded home twenty-five lengths ahead.

Longden had pushed him out to an eight-length lead at the half-mile. They had twelve after a mile. When they were done, they'd shaved two-fifths of a second off of War Admiral's record for that race, finishing the mile and a half in 2:28-1/5.

Count Fleet had filled out. He was now one thousand pounds of muscle. His running style fit Longden's riding too. Longden had a vigorous hand-riding technique, but he would not whip a horse. He never took his stick to Count Fleet.

AND HE wasn't taking his stick to George Royal, either. He was last.

Jack Murphy had written in the *San Diego Union*: "One can only wish Longden had the theatrical flair of Ted Williams. Williams quit with a home run in Boston's Fenway Park. . . . Longden's chances of quitting a winner are so remote that Santa Anita management has scheduled special ceremonies honoring the gaffer Monday, closing day of the meeting."

It looked like Murphy would be right. George Royal showed no signs of the acceleration he would need to catch the horses up front. He was, as the chart said, racing on his own courage.

The field thundered by the grandstand and the clubhouse, Plaque in front by two lengths, followed by Polar Sea, who was still looking game.

By the time they had run a mile, Longden had shuffled George Royal up to seventh. But he'd passed only quickly fading horses. The real stuff was still ahead.

The San Juan Capistrano is a long race, about a mile and three-quarters over the turf. A tired field hit the backstretch. Around the stretch turn, Longden had worked his way up to fifth. He was running on the far outside. The favorite, Hill Rise, was hanging with him. They were hooked up in the middle of the pack, running at each other's throatlatches. There was a lot of horse in front of them. Plaque was headstrong on the lead. Or Et Argent was still running good, up in third. Polar Sea was still pushing Plaque, forcing his hand.

"A WHIP doesn't make a horse run," Longden had said. "If you're doing your best and somebody's hitting you, you're going to sulk."

Bill Christine wrote about Longden in the *Los Angeles Times*: "'Johnny had some tricks,' said Jerry Lambert, who rode against him many times in California. 'He did what he had to do to win races. He'd send a horse, and then when you tried to close some ground, he'd back up his horse right into your face.'

"After a race in which he was outridden by a victorious Longden, Ray York said, 'You can get to him—you just can't get by him.'"

Longden was a master of the false pace. He'd send his horse like a rabbit out to the front, and he'd make a big show of riding the horse, as if he were pushing him on. In fact he'd be rating the horse, holding him back.

The competition would come up on him, and he'd let the horse out. Suddenly there was another gear, a gear nobody thought was available.

Kevin Modesti quoted Longden on this technique in the *Los Angeles Daily News*: "When I was easing my horse back and rating him, I pretended to be going all out with him," he explained. "Other jocks thought I was using him too soon, while actually I was giving him a breather and saving something for the final part of it. Sure, there is a lot of bluff in riding this way, and you're taking a gamble. But more often than not it worked for me. When other horses came to me, I'd just open up on them."

Longden had gotten his start in the bush leagues, where the cowboys do anything they have to do to get under the wire first, and he never stopped race riding. He told Nick Canepa of the *San Diego Tribune*, "When I first rode, there were no cameras and no photo finish. You could get away with a lot more than you can now."

On September 3, 1956, the Pumper pushed home his 4,871st winner, and became the world's winningest rider. He had broken the record set by British jock Sir Gordon Richards.

He wasn't done.

He was sitting on George Royal, after all, with a job to get done. His famous techniques had nothing to do with the way he was riding now. Coming to the turn he was stuck with Hill Rise in the middle of the pack—George Royal and Hill Rise were moving together. They picked up the pace and suddenly were improving position. The two horses, Hill Rise the money favorite and George Royal the sentimental one, made a strong move on the turn. Plaque was still up there in front after a mile and three-eighths. He was showing incredible sticking power. After all this slogging through the turf, after the six-furlong run downhill, and the pressure from Polar Sea, Plaque was still loose on front. Plaque was still game.

George Royal shook Hill Rise on the turn. Hill Rise faded. The Pumper had ridden his horse right up into the race. When George Royal and Longden ranged up on Plaque, Plaque shook off Polar Sea. Now it was the two of them. Plaque and Ussery had owned this race. George Royal and Johnny Longden had come on to take it. Let's go, said Ussery. And at the top of the stretch they went.

Plaque was on the inside, and George Royal was out on the track. George Royal had come on like a storm in the final yards of the turn. Plaque was tenacious. They were right at each other. Neck and neck. The crowd was screaming for Longden.

Johnny Longden (right) and Willie Shoemaker (left) after
Longden's hairbreadth victory on George Royal in the San Juan
Capistrano at Santa Anita: Longden goes out a winner.

Joe Hernandez was calling the race—he had been Longden's
agent in 1931—but no one could hear the PA over the crowd.
Everyone was screaming for Longden as they came tearing
down the stretch. Only Longden was cool, hand-riding George
Royal all the way—no whip. Ussery was whipping the hell out
of Plaque. They went on together. All down the stretch they
were at each other.

At the wire, George Royal surged.

Longden got it by a breath.

The crowd went absolutely nuts. Longden waved excitedly when he returned to the winner's circle. 6,032! His last. "What a gratifying win," he said. "The greatest race of my life."

"Old man!" shouted an old jock. "You rode the hair off that horse!"

Willie Shoemaker walked into the press conference following the race and threw his arms around Longden. He had once sung a song to Longden at the annual jockey's ball:

Hang up your tack, John Longden,
Hang up your tack and quit.
Hang up your tack, John Longden,
Pack up your bit and git.

Now he said, "John, you're the greatest."

Longden went on to train horses for years. Just three years after his retirement, in 1969, he trained Majestic Prince to victory in the Kentucky Derby and the Preakness. He is the only horseman to both ride and train a Derby winner.

Johnny Longden's statue is in the paddock at Santa Anita, next to those of the California riders who eventually surpassed his record: Willie Shoemaker and Lafitte Pincay.

Johnny Longden died at ninety-six, on Valentine's Day, 2003.

7
Race of the Century

New York City in the era following World War II seems to have operated with an almost Stalinist disregard for the aesthetic and historic qualities of its buildings. The attitude seems not just negligent but rather malicious. Artistic considerations were chucked in favor of an invented idealism regarding what might best suit the urban environment. Thus Gropius's horrible wedge of sooty glass now called the Met Life building, finished in 1963, does as much to block the vista that once was the long view up Park Avenue as it does to destroy the appeal of the buildings around it, looming over the Helmsley and Grand Central, replacing sky light with poured concrete and shadows. The granite base looks like a prison for automobiles; the octagonal tower looks mammoth and brutal. The thing is, of course, that's what they wanted: that school of architecture is even called Brutalist (derived from the French *béton brut*, or "raw concrete"). It's marked by repetition and regularity, as well as a bizarre display of the function of the building itself (water tanks, parking lots) rather than a person's relationship to the building—which I guess is a kind of large-scale, objective solipsism. The school has been loathed since its worst buildings went up.

I don't think the basement currently operating as Penn Station belongs to an architectural movement, but I am sure if it does, it shouldn't. The station is an endless system of underground tubes filled with a seemingly random assortment of vendors selling panty hose, newspapers, and twenty-four-ounce cans of beer from giant tubs filled with ice. For those of you in the mood for a drink at the bar or a hamburger, we've got a Houlihan's sunk into the wall over there. Need some deodorant? Ah, the Duane Reade drugstore. Penn Station has to be one of the most embarrassing moments in a city that provides plenty of opportunity for embarrassment. That we leave it to this warren of piped music and dirty tiles to say "Welcome to New York" is just shy of disgraceful. A quick comparison to Grand Central pushes it over the edge.

The destruction of the old Penn Station was a cap of sorts to this desecration of the city and serves as a classic example of the ridiculous myopia of that era of urban planning. The original Penn Station was a wonderful McKim, Meade, and White building, bigger than any building ever built for rail travel and covering more than eight acres between Thirty-first and Thirty-third Street at Seventh Avenue. The waiting room was designed after Roman baths and was 277 feet long. It was a grand structure all around, with statues of eagles and glass arcades, honeycomb ceilings and brass handrails. (Of course, they had demolished something like 500 buildings to build it, so it could be said that the pattern of disregard had begun much earlier.) The painful, slow demolition of the original

Penn Station between 1962 and 1966 is said to have spawned the historical preservation movement.

Not in time to save the old New York racetracks, however. For in the fifties, New York City turned to its tracks the same brutal pragmatism it had employed throughout the city. What charm we have at New York's contemporary centers for racing comes from the racing. The connections to history are few—as if the New York Racing Association (NYRA) shipped all the historical sensibility up to Saratoga.

After the state's racing ban of 1910 was lifted in 1913, only four of New York's many tracks reopened. Saratoga, Belmont, Jamaica, and Aqueduct had all survived the attempt by Governor Charles Hughes and state legislators to outlaw gambling on horse racing.

These were very different tracks. Saratoga was a resort town. Belmont was a massive construction, a premier track, and the invention of very rich men who had conceived it to be the most lavish track in America. Jamaica had been built nearby Belmont Park but had been constructed in the populist spirit by the Metropolitan Jockey Club. This was probably New York's most popular track until it closed in the late fifties.

Aqueduct opened September 27, 1894, in Ozone Park, Queens. The media guide for the track informs us that the six-furlong track "was built on a 23-acre site with a boardwalk instead of a lawn and seating for 2,000. Less than 700 people and six bookmakers are on hand for opening day." The track was an outlaw track, started without sanction from racing's governing bodies. Aqueduct remained unsanctioned for only one year, until the fall of 1895, when the Jockey Club recognized the track.

Tugboat Skipper William Carter then endowed the track's first big handicap race—the Carter Handicap—run to this day.

In the mid-1950s, New York state legislators and parts of the racing community got together and decided that New York racing needed help. To maintain the level of racing that New York had seen, and to preserve its illustrious history, they would unify the tracks under a state-sanctioned, nonprofit bureaucracy. They called their new entity the Greater New York Association (GNYA). Later, they changed the name to the New York Racing Association, as it is still known.

Ron Hale wrote, in his essay "A Short History of New York Tracks":

> One by one, shareholders of the four tracks racing in New York sold out to the GNYA. Saratoga accepted $102 per share; Jamaica accepted $325 a share; Belmont accepted $91 per share; and finally Aqueduct accepted $183 per share on September 7, 1955. The GNYA was officially in business. The first step was to rebuild Aqueduct on its present site into a megatrack. When the $33-million track reopened in the fall of 1959 for a 66-day meeting, all records were broken. The track was referred to as New Aqueduct to distinguish it from the same track at the same location that had opened in 1894. That track was now referred to as "Old Aqueduct." With the opening of "new" Aqueduct, Jamaica was torn down.

Like Penn Station or the Met Life building, little of the new Aqueduct was given over to aesthetics. The bureaucracy that now ran New York racing was confident that the slab concrete building, as direct in its invention as it was in its expression, was the answer. It lacked the modernist flair of Arlington, if for no other reason than it had been built thirty-odd years later, and that that flair was no longer stylish. I know of only one piece of the old Aqueduct that was saved: a pole on the stretch called the Man o' War pole.

In 1920, Man o' War came to race at Aqueduct, having just run in the Stuyvesant Handicap out at the old Jamaica Park. He had carried thirty-five pounds of added weight over the horse Yellow Hand, which chased him to the wire to place. Even handicapped by such a burden, Man o' War won it by eight lengths. With Man o' War, it isn't a matter of recording how he finished; in all but one race, it's simply a matter of recording the size of his victory.

As the 1920 season continued, most horsemen gave up on racing against Man o' War. Sam Riddle and trainer Louis Feustel ran him as they could, even if only two horses showed up. He won one race, the Lawrence, by a hundred lengths. There was only one other horse in the race.

The Whitneys' trainer, James Rowe, Jr., called Man o' War "That Red Lobster" when everyone else called him Big Red. He believed the horse was beatable. He had his horse John P. Grier tuned up and ready to roll for the 1920 Dwyer Stakes at the old Aqueduct. His sights were set on taking down Big Red.

Man o' War was a brilliantly fast horse once he got rolling. He was left at the gate a few times over his career and still managed to get under the wire well in front. More often, he simply had the race from start to finish.

At the start of the Dwyer, Man o' War went, and John P. Grier went with him. Miraculously, considering it was Man o'

War the horse had engaged, Grier would not fold. The game horse stayed with Man o' War for over a mile, and at the eighth pole Grier pulled a nose in front. Big Red probably couldn't believe it, and anyway it didn't last long. By the sixteenth, Big Red had caught Grier and roared past him. He won the race in 1:49-1/5 for the mile and an eighth, setting a new American record—and is said to have broken Grier's heart, whatever that means.

Supposedly they've saved either the eighth or the sixteenth pole at Aqueduct. I've heard both stories. Either they kept the moment where James P. Grier got a nose in front of Man o' War, which certainly would be worth saving, or they saved the sixteenth, where the attempt was rebuffed. Whether it's the eighth pole or the sixteenth hardly matters—it's a good story. But the NYRA had been formed to preserve the history of these great tracks and these great races, and this pole is but a tiny nod. Keeping an old pole while you tear down two tracks hardly seems like a historical preservation movement.

Aqueduct today is like a subway station. It can feel, on a grim day, like an extension of its parking lot. It exists only to fulfill; it's an expression of its purpose. In this sense it is some of the purest modernism I've ever dealt with. Mostly, like at the UN for instance, you see a lot of the pretense of functionality warped into a baroque expression of a modernist visual ideal. No such mistakes were made at Aqueduct. That place is as clean of ornament as an empty sidewalk at 3:30 P.M. on a bitter winter's day. Which is often exactly what it feels like. Actually, that's often enough what it is—an empty winter sidewalk. Which is to say that it's not very clean of anything but people. Plenty of chewing gum ground into the concrete, no people.

In 1976, Aqueduct completed its journey to the track we have today by opening a "winterized" inner track. The winterized track dries quickly so it won't freeze. The turns are tight. This allows for horses to run forty miles an hour in the freezing cold while the wind whips and little icicles cling to the rail. A couple of thousand people will come to Aqueduct on an average day in the winter. They'll sit inside and watch pretty cheap horses run for light purses. All the big horses have been shipped off to sunnier climes, and all the big money has gone with them.

It's hard to see winter racing at Aqueduct as the sport of kings. This is the land of hard-luck punters, West Indians shouting at the jockeys, old Chinese men chain-smoking and poring over the simulcasting programs. The bitter wind is constant, and the racing is often canceled because of blizzards or cold. In a *New York* magazine feature on winter racing at the Big A, jockey C. C. Lopez lamented, "It's unbelievable. You're out there in nothing but a leotard and a T-shirt. Your hands freeze, your feet freeze, your face freezes. The horse is going 40 miles an hour into a gale—what's the wind-chill on that?"

It is generally thought that if a horse gets out front on this bullring track, he wins. To say that it tends to favor front-funners is historically an understatement.

Here's my problem: I love Aqueduct. It is, for instance, one of the only tracks where the clubhouse apron affords a decent view of the stretch run, because the apron is tilted, like a stage, and you actually look down on the track. At most tracks the clubhouse side is where the floor will be tiled with something a little shinier than the poured concrete of the grandstand side,

The paddock at Aqueduct.

the bathrooms will have been cleaned more recently, and the lines at the betting windows will be shorter. It's the better side to bring company to; it's where you'll want to introduce people to racing, if not up in the restaurant or in a box. Those who prefer not to hang out with Rastafarians who scream obscenities at the jockeys after every race might want to drift over to the clubhouse side. Women seem to prefer it. What you sacrifice, especially if you like the rail, is the view. The horses are all running at you. You are standing after the finish line, so all of the desperate bump and hustle of the last seventy yards looks like a herd of horses running straight at you—in other words, indecipherable. But at Aqueduct they figured out the line of sight and solved the problem.

An even better innovation is the paddock, which is built right under your feet at the rail. It's one story down, with a fence around the mezzanine upon which you can lean.

I like to look at the paddock, and I like the stretch run, and it's the only track I've been to where I can do both without moving from my railbird position on the clubhouse side.

Brilliant.

Practical, yes. The scene at the Big A is certainly nothing, atmosphere wise, to compare to the spinning ceiling fans and striped awnings up at the Spa. But it's fun. I love it.

I love it for the same reasons I criticize it. It's all about horse racing. It's not about gardening (most of the year it's freezing, after all). It's not about lapel pins. It's not about centennial passes, or charity balls, or horse auctions.

Aqueduct is direct.

It's horse racing.

Three of the best horses of the sixties, if not three of the best horses of all time, made very serious contributions to their careers at the Big A. Buckpasser ran at Aqueduct seventeen times and won twelve of those—he was Horse of the Year in 1966. Dr. Fager ran the seven-furlong Vosburgh in 1:20-1/5 and set a track record in 1968. That year he was Horse of the Year; he was also top sprinter, top grass horse, and top handicap horse. Think about that: the sprint, the turf, and the handicap divisions dominated by the same horse. Damascus, one of the last of the great Belair horses, 1967 Horse of the Year, raced at Aqueduct. In the Woodward

Stakes of 1967, all three were called to the post. One race, and in it, the 1966, 1967, and 1968 horses of the year, with, among them, twelve divisional championships. The race was rightly billed as the race of the century.

BUCKPASSER was racing royalty. He was foaled at Claiborne Farm in 1963. The 1953 Horse of the Year, Tom Fool, was his sire, and War Admiral's stakes-winning daughter Busanda was his dam. Busanda, as if it wasn't enough to be sired by War Admiral and therefore granddaughter of Man o' War, was also out of a mare by Blue Larkspur, the 1929 Belmont Stakes winner and Horse of the Year. Back a little farther up the family tree, one finds the two-time Horse of the Year, the chocolate soldier Equipose. Tough acts to follow, all of them.

But Buckpasser was up to it. He was perhaps the most perfectly conformed horse to ever hit the track. Horses, because they have been observed so closely for so long, have become more a catalog of errors than anything else. They generally have dozens upon dozens of tiny imperfections that a trained eye can locate and evaluate. Buckpasser was said to have none. What's more, he was gentle and well mannered. When Richard Stone Reeves painted his Horse of the Year portrait, he reportedly said that if Buckpasser had been able to talk, he certainly would have invited Reeves into the stall with the offer of a cocktail and a comfortable seat.

Buckpasser lost on his first trip around the track but took his next two. In his first stakes race he developed his style, the dramatic stretch run typical of a true classic distance horse.

Buckpasser's three-year-old career was stupendous. Eddie Neloy picked up training responsibilities from Bill Winfrey. By the end of the year, Buckpasser notched victories in thirteen of fourteen starts. At the Flamingo Stakes at Hialeah, the management decided to run the race as an exhibition in order to avoid the negative betting pools guaranteed by such an overwhelming favorite. Red Smith dubbed it "The Chicken Flamingo." Buckpasser uncharacteristically grabbed the early lead and then seemed to grow bored. He was better at catching horses, it seems, than he was at staying in front of them. Abe's Hope made a move and even got out in front, opening up two lengths before Buckpasser found another gear (or renewed interest) and exploded. With incredible heart and a few quick, long strides, he blew past the challenger and took the race.

When Buckpasser developed a quarter crack, he missed the Kentucky Derby and the early summer races. He returned to the track the day of the Belmont Stakes, but he was running in a short allowance (a limited distance, and not a stakes race), seeing if he still had it in him. He did. He broke the track record winning the American Derby. Then he went on a rampage: the Chicago Stakes, the Brooklyn Derby, the Woodward Stakes, the Travers Stakes, the Malibu Stakes, the Brooklyn Handicap, the Lawrence, and the two-mile-long Jockey Club Gold Cup. By the end of his three-year-old career he had won more than a million dollars. He was a shoo-in for 1966 Horse of the Year.

As a four-year-old, Buckpasser carried a lot of weight. Handicapping really kicks in at four. Most races for three-year-olds are run under a single weight, or with small allowances (nonwinners given a few pounds, say). But the big four-year-old handicap races are weighted at the discretion of track officials. Their goal is to even the contest. A faster horse will be weighted with pieces of lead. A horse as fast as Buckpasser will carry much more weight than the rest of the ponies in the gate. The idea is to make the race more sporting—and a better betting proposition—but it frequently has wretched repercussions. Many lesser horses have gotten a nose in front of a champion and earned an undeserved victory because the champ had lead in the saddle. In the Suburban Handicap, Buckpasser carried twenty-two pounds more than the horse that was running down the stretch in front. Seventy yards from the wire Ring Twice was two lengths out. Buckpasser kicked by him and won by half a length. In his next outing, the Brooklyn Handicap, he was again heavily weighted, but this time he didn't have the strength to get past the lightly weighted horse running out front. His next stop would be the Big A and the Woodward Stakes, the Race of the Century.

AFTER William Woodward, Sr., owner of Belair Stud and Gallant Fox, died in 1953, the farm went to his son, William Woodward, Jr. Sunny Jim Fitzsimmons was still on the payroll as trainer, and together they campaigned the great Nashua. William Woodward, Jr., would not be long for this world, however. In 1955 Woodward and his wife Ann came home from a party for the Duchess of Windsor, at which the rash of recent burglaries throughout the North Shore of Long Island was much discussed. They both were sleeping with weapons beside their beds, he with a revolver, and she with a twelve-gauge loaded for duck. At 3 A.M., Ann was awakened by her dog, heard a noise, kicked open her door, and unloaded both barrels. One of the blasts took out her husband. It was scandal. Tongues wagged. "Nothing like a murder in the country to cure what ails you," said the Duchess of Windsor. Truman Capote and Dominick Dunne wrote about the story. A grand jury was convened. The jurors deliberated for only thirty minutes and decided that Ann had acted without malice. The law would consider the shooting an accident, and she was exonerated. But she couldn't shake the black mark on her reputation. With Capote's story in the hopper at *Esquire*, and after a particularly rough argument with her son, she poisoned herself. Elsie Woodward said, "Well, that's that; she shot my son and Truman has just murdered her, and so now I suppose we don't have to worry about that anymore."

Edith Bancroft, Jr.'s sister, inherited the Belair Silks and a couple of horses, and retained the services of Sunny Jim. Most of the horses, including Nashua, were dispersed. Mrs. Bancroft boarded her horses at Jonabell Farm, near Lexington, and it was there on April 14, 1964, that Damascus hit the ground.

Frank Whitely, Jr., campaigned Damascus to twenty-one wins in thirty-two starts. He finished off the board only once. In 1967 he won the Travers by twenty-two lengths, after notching victories in the the Preakness, the Belmont, the Dwyer, and the American Derby. He was Three-Year-Old of the Year, Handicap Horse of the Year, and Horse of the Year.

DR. FAGER was homebred at William McKnight's Tartan Stable. He got his name from a neurosurgeon who saved the life of trainer John Nerud after Nerud took a spill from a pony.

A strong contingent believes Dr. Fager, not Secretariat or Man o' War, deserves the title as the greatest horse of all time. It's an absurd argument, not because an answer is obvious but because the solution is impossible. Still, it gives you a sense of the horse. Dr. Fager was astonishing. In twenty-two starts he won nineteen times.

His two-year-old career was dominating but for one poorly run race in which he placed behind champion juvenile Successor. As a four-year-old in 1968, Dr. Fager was unstoppable. First, after a bad start and carrying 134 pounds, he coasted to an eight-length victory at Arlington and ran a mile in 1:32-1/5, a world record. In September that year he raced for the first time on the grass in the United Nations Handicap. He was assigned 134 pounds, giving 16 to the future Horse of the Year and turf champ Fort Marcy and to the Australian champion import Tobin Bronze. The track was soft and slippery. Dr. Fager didn't flinch; he got up in the race and fought the pace all the way, finally pulling ahead to take it. In the last race of his career, the 1968 Vosburgh, he carried 139 pounds, set a track record for seven furlongs, and won the race by six lengths.

Only three horses ever beat Dr. Fager. Successor was the first. The other two were Buckpasser and Damascus.

TO SEE any one of these horses run would be a treat, to see a matchup—and there were a few matchups between these rivals—would be wonderful. To see them all called to the post is incredible. Going into the Woodward, these three horses had won forty-eight of fifty-eight starts. The Race of the Century.

55,259 people showed up at the Big A, along with six horses. With the great three came three other horses. Handsome Boy was in the running. Most under discussion was the fact that two of the other three horses were coupled entries, meaning that one trainer had entered both. Damascus's trainer had entered a horse named Hedevar. Coupled with Buckpasser was a horse named Great Power. There was then, and has been ever since, much discussion of the use of these rabbits. Frank Whiteley claimed that his horse, Hedevar, had good reason to be in the race. The *Blood Horse* quoted him as saying, "Hell, Hedevar is no rabbit or whatever they're calling him." From the same article "Whiteley pointed out that his 5-year-old once was co-holder of the world's mile record, that he runs best when fresh, and had just come back from a summer layoff with a win, and deserved a shot." It's a very hard sell indeed that Whiteley believed that Hedevar honestly had a shot, but at least he stuck to his guns.

Edward Neloy, trainer of Buckpasser, was just as forthright about using his horse, Great Power, to influence the pace.

John Nerud complained.

Alfred G. Vanderbilt felt the need to be heard. "I want to go on record," he told the *Blood Horse*, "I'd like to see just the four of them—Buckpasser, Dr. Fager, Damascus, and Handsome Boy—in there."

None of the punters gave anyone but the big three any action. Among those three, however, the public was divided.

Buckpasser went off at 8-5, the two three-year-olds were 9-5. The coupled entries were represented with the same odds as the favored horses, but the odds on Handsome Boy were 10-1.

All six horses broke sharply. Dr. Fager got out front, Buckpasser and Damascus settled immediately to the back of the pack.

Ron Turcotte, in the irons on Hedevar, hustled his horse, gave chase, and applied pressure on the front-running Dr. Fager down the first run by the grandstand.

Most jockeys holler when the horses break. When the bell rings and the gates flip open, all the jocks urge the horses, the horses leap, and everyone yells. Bobby Ussery, up on Great Power, did some early race riding and took the typical commotion further. He set the whip to his horse immediately and hollered at the top of his lungs. With a mile and an eighth to go, Ussery was riding as if he were gunning for the wire.

Dr. Fager's jockey said later that all the shouting and the whipping of Great Power at the start of the race had upset Dr. Fager, but he admitted that he had used these tactics himself. Dr. Fager was naturally a fractious horse, hard to handle and eager, and Great Power had successfully unsettled him. The pressure from Hedevar and Great Power pushed him through the early splits.

By the time they settled in for the run around the first turn, it was clear that even if Ussery whipped Great Power all the way around the track, he'd never make it. He was already dragging.

Hedevar was strong on the inside. Dr. Fager had a head out front, barreling along beside him around that first turn.

Great Power continued to fade. By the time the horses covered a half-mile, Great Power had begun already the waning and weakening that would land him in dead last, some fifty lengths off the lead.

Handsome Boy was sitting in the middle of the pack in fourth, where he would remain for the entire race, the drama unfolding around him having no spurring or discouraging effect on this plodder.

Hedevar took the lead back from Dr. Fager as the two horses hit the backstretch.

Damascus, agile, light, with a powerful hind-end and rippling muscle, now made his move. Buckpasser was hooked up with Damascus, and Braulio Baeza, Buckpasser's jock, was left no choice: go with him or never catch him. He went with him. Great Power was falling past as the two classic closers settled into their champion styles at the back of the field.

Dr. Fager was a monster on the front. He's a miler, he's a sprinter, he's everything. He's a blazing speed machine, without mercy. He took the lead back from Hedevar, and Hedevar too began to fade.

By the time they'd run a mile, things looked very different.

Damascus had been a dozen lengths off the lead coming into the stretch turn. He and Buckpasser had rolled together, tearing around the turn. It was clear that the two closers were going to catch the tiring Dr. Fager, but who would win? Would Dr. Fager crumble? Would he repel the challenge? If he caved in, Buckpasser and Damascus were stride for stride, and had been practically the whole race.

The Shoe was up on Damascus and was riding an incredible race, keeping his horse focused and saving ground. Baeza on Buckpasser was following his lead.

Then Damascus turned it on.

Damascus ranged up on Dr. Fager. The good doctor stuck for a moment. Dr. Fager wasn't supposed to get beat, and he dug in. But after the race he'd run, crazed out front and pressured by rabbits, his weakening was inevitable: he folded.

From the *Blood Horse*: "The peculiar fractions of 22-2/5, 22-4/5, 24, 26-2/5, and 25 told an interesting story. While Dr. Fager was running that slow fourth quarter, Damascus was running it in 24-3/5, and within that quarter was an even more remarkable furlong."

Damascus blew by Dr. Fager and left Buckpasser in his wake. The Shoe had hit the switch: Damascus was exploding like a bomb. He was stretched out, low to the ground, running like a machine. He opened up daylight on the horses up the track. Coming into the stretch, he already had five lengths on them. By the time he hit the wire Damascus had opened ten lengths.

Buckpasser was still coming up on Dr. Fager, and the Doc stuck again. But again he folded. He was tired, he'd been run into the ground, but he gave all he had. Buckpasser caught Dr. Fager only in the last yards of the race. Even then, he struggled by the tiring Dr. Fager to get a length and a half past him.

Of Damascus and his explosive closing move: "He's quick as a cat," said the Shoe. He told the *Blood Horse*, "I've always been kind of high on him. I hate to praise any horse too much—you open your mouth and find you've put your foot in it—but he's improving in all his races. I guess he's as good a horse as I ever rode."

There in the winner's circle at Aqueduct—the new Aqueduct, all poured concrete and pragmatic style—stood representatives of one of racing's most established stables. William Woodward III, William Woodward's daughter Edith Bancroft, and her husband Thomas Bancroft, stood with Whitely and the Shoe, happily gripping the cup presented as a trophy in the race named after William Woodward, Sr.

8
A Good Cigar, Where the Turf Meets the Surf

P erhaps it's a piece of nationalistic faux nostalgia that I'm stuck with, but in twentieth-
century American history I can locate three perfect construc-
tions, three fabrications of atmosphere that were orchestrated
flawlessly and masterminded to create the best possible party.
Some moment in the early sixties at Hugh Hefner's mansion
must have been about as good as it gets. I imagine playing
pool with Cary Grant while sipping martinis, a glowing, sul-
try bunny at my side. We'd make perfect jokes and listen to
the strains of music and laughter from the next room. The
bunny and I slip off to the grotto. . . . The Rat Pack in Vegas was mostly illusion—Dino famously sober, faking it for
all. "I spill more than he drinks," said Sinatra. But even the
illusion has become the bedrock of sophisticated lushness.
These guys wrapped up in their impenetrable camaraderie
like musketeers of Jack Daniel's on the rocks: all cufflinks,
shoeshines, and talent.

These first two party scenes have a lot in common. They are set in astonishingly permissive places, for one thing. In Vegas and at the Playboy Mansion, anything goes. Anything. You can flirt, love, gamble, drink, it's okay. According to the mythos of these places, unlike the befouled streets of the French Quarter, you won't end up passed out in the gutter, or in jail. You'll just get cooler and cooler. The more you participate, the better you'll get at it, and the better your tuxedo will fit. Above even the permission to do whatever you want, however, comes the permission to be *whomever* you want. You will be unfettered by your typical hesitations, inhibitions, or clumsiness with dance steps and words. The men at these parties are all talented, intelligent, well dressed, and rich. The women are all beautiful, sexy, witty, and available. It's a transparent American fantasy. The problem with these two examples, of course, is that they are long gone.

The third party is more distinct, more accessible, and—lucky for us—ongoing. It too was invented back in the days when men wore hats. In Southern California, about half an hour north of San Diego, a hundred miles south of Los Angeles, the surf meets the turf at the Del Mar Thoroughbred Club.

Inland, among the rolling cowboy hills of the upmarket Rancho Santa Fe, citrus trees shade the scrub, and horses kick up the dust. You drive narrow, twisting roads, deeper and deeper into the desert. It's been developed since its true heyday, but it remains great country. It's not a part of Southern California one usually thinks of. This is MexiCali, cowboy country. You can easily imagine the ghost of John Wayne up on a hilltop on horseback, swaggering along next to Ronald Reagan.

The Pacific Coast Highway hugs the shoreline. It winds through the hills that abut the beach, and one is always cresting a piney ridge and having a vista unfurled in front of the windshield. Beach town after beach town: Solano Beach, Encinitas, Carlsbad.

The highway turns into a main street in each of these little villages, the roadside lined with Pacific-themed hotels, Mexican restaurants, and surf shops. They are lovely, relaxed towns. Some of them are richer than others, and they have slight variations of town mission. Some lean to the villa-and-wine-bar motif, others are ripped from the tracks of *Endless Summer*.

In between the towns, where the hills open up to beautiful views of the blue ocean, the coast is dotted with campgrounds and public beaches.

Blondes of both sexes besiege the entire coast. Everyone is absurdly healthy. Eastern city dwellers beware: I felt like a pasty, blobbish, overdressed convalescent everywhere I went. Folks zing along the shoulders of the highway on expensive bicycles. Groups of tan, young surfers are always getting in and out of wonderful old trucks, chopped Volkswagen microbuses, or rumbling, ancient Chevy Silverados, all of them covered with stickers. Shirtless boys with long hair and a dope-smoke smile glinting dully in their eyes, girls in bikini tops and shorts, carry their carved, waxed, painted surfboards to the ocean where they will loll in the surf like some strange species of beautiful seal. Bobbing, pointed the same direction, too far out for us to hear if they're even talking to one another, they wait for the wave.

morning is grey, but the clouds burn off by 10 A.M., ...и from then on the California sun never ceases to shine until in the late evening it casts beautiful sparkles of reflection across the crests of the tide, and finally sinks into the ocean, inspiring thousands of surfboard paintings and album covers. If it ever comes up—secession, perhaps—I recommend that California ditch the bear on the state flag and go for the fat red sun sinking into the pacific, à la the Japanese. The salt air comes in off the Pacific in soft steady streams and friendly gusts. It tousles your hair and fills the lungs with healthful effulgence. You breathe deeper, your complexion begins to glow, and you relish the slow roll of the sand between your toes. Finding another fish taco or, better yet, a good margarita comes to seem like a good project worth most of the day, as long as it doesn't involve doing anything too strenuous (or take time away from the racing).

In the middle of this capital C California is the town of Del Mar. Driving along the Pacific Coast Highway, from Carlsbad where I was staying, the hills parted for the first time, and I saw this Spanish mission complex, this wonderful adobe-colored, red-tile-roofed spread, with a mission bell and numerous buildings. I almost drove the rental car into the ocean in my excitement.

People who go to the races only at Del Mar would probably shrivel and die on the spot if taken to Pimlico for an afternoon in the fall.

William Murray, the *New Yorker* writer, novelist, and track bum, wrote the great little paperback for Del Mar, titled *Del Mar: Its Life and Good Times*, the text of which is taken mainly

Bing Crosby helps launch Del Mar by taking tickets.

from his book *The Wrong Horse.* He quotes Oscar Otis: "What this is, it's more of a mood, a way of life. It's racing, all right, but with this important difference—it's a great place to relax." Murray goes on to say, "Nobody in the world was more relaxed than Bing Crosby, so it seems entirely appropriate that he should have been the one to launch the place, more than sixty-five years ago."

It is my suspicion that Bing Crosby, though certainly still very well known, has undergone an adjustment of reputation. "White Christmas," changing social connotations about pipe smoking and hats (his two trademark affectations), and the advent of rock and roll all conspire to make him appear less hip than he was.

Crosby scored 38 No. 1 hits—the Beatles had 24, Elvis 18. As a solo recording artist, he shot 368 records to the charts before 1962, tacking on another 28 as a vocalist with a bandleader. Sinatra sent 209, Elvis 149, and Nat King Cole 118.

Bing Crosby starred in fifty-five movies from 1932 through 1971, plus some shorts and cameos, and some two dozen of those movies were among the top ten box-office hits. At year end, when the money was counted in Hollywood, Bing was among the top ten box-office stars at least fifteen times. From 1944 to 1948, he was the top box-office draw in America.

Crosby was influenced early by jazz and had serious friendships with serious jazzmen. "The thing you have to understand about Bing Crosby," Artie Shaw famously said, "was that he was the first hip white person born in the United States."

Crosby was among the first to utilize the power of recorded music, which allowed the vocalist to relax. Rather than hollering over the band to be heard, or singing only in the high registers so as to pierce the sound of the band, with amplification and recording Crosby could deliver a smooth, laid-back croon, among the first of its kind.

In an interview with George Varga for the *San Diego Union-Tribune* in 1997, Tony Bennett said: "I call myself a 'Bing Crosby singer.' I was very influenced by Bing. I liked the essence of Bing. He made us all a living; he showed us all how to communicate as popular singers by relaxing." On PBS in 1999, Bennett observed: "Just imagine something five times stronger than the popularity of Elvis Presley and the Beatles put together. Bing Crosby dominated all of the airwaves. He was the only guy who had hour shows on radio stations, where other artists would just have one record played."

Sammy Davis, Jr., once missed his cue five times in a row while recording with Crosby and Sinatra. When Sinatra asked him what was wrong, Davis answered: "To hell with you, Frank, I'm listening to Bing Crosby!"

Sinatra, too, was a fan. "Bing's death is almost more than I can take." Sinatra said when Crosby died. "He was the father of my career, the idol of my youth and a dear friend of my maturity. His passing leaves a gaping hole in our music and in the lives of everybody who ever loved him. And that's just about everybody. Thank God we have his films and his records providing us with his warmth and talent forever."

When they lived in the Dakota in New York, Yoko gave John Lennon an antique bubble Wurlitzer, and Lennon filled it with Bing Crosby records.

All of which is to say that Bing Crosby was no square. He was a very cool cucumber, the original crooner, and wildly popular. He had spent a couple of nights in jail and many a night out on the town. Most of all he loved to sing. Germane to our story: he loved horse racing.

IN 1926, Del Mar was a small town with a golf course. Then a hurricane smacked the links, and Del Mar was just a small town with a waterlogged, unusable piece of ground. The golf course was officially closed in 1930.

In 1933, the Twenty-second Congressional District of California was looking to build permanent fairgrounds with support from the WPA. Pari-mutuel wagering had just been legalized in California, and the fairgrounds were to have a racetrack. The waterlogged golf course looked like the perfect spot.

Bing Crosby had recorded his first solo hit—"I Surrender Dear"—in 1931. He was in his first movie, *The Big Broadcast*, in 1932.

Crosby was flush. He bought a spread in Rancho Santa Fe, a historic piece of the original Rancho Don Juan Osuna. Don Juan had been the first mayor of Mexican San Diego in 1835. He patrolled the gritty streets in a long black robe, with a powdered wig on his head and an official tassled walking staff in hand. His land, originally more than 8,000 acres, had been parceled, just as Bing Crosby's has now. Today the Crosby estate in Rancho Santa Fe includes a golf course and 722 acres on which 443 homes are or will be built. There remain 190 acres of permanent open space.

William A. Quigley knew Crosby loved horse racing, and knew he lived in the area, so he approached Crosby and asked if he might care to form a syndicate to run racing at the Del Mar fairgrounds. At Warner Brothers in Burbank, Crosby, his brother, Gary Cooper, and Pat O'Brien met with Quigley and others to form the Del Mar Turf Club. Stock was issued at one hundred dollars a share, and they leased the racetrack from the Twenty-second District.

When the money for the building ran out, Crosby and Pat O'Brien borrowed against their life insurance policies to get more.

The exotic paddock at Del Mar.

Architects Sam and Joe Hamill built a wonderland. They copied major landmarks of the Spanish Colonial Southwest and built the track buildings all within a stone's throw of each other. Nancy Stout noted in her book *Home Stretch* that "The atmosphere at Del Mar has always promoted a sense of entertainment. Before museums and theme parks routinely created replicas of historic villages, there was Del Mar."

One building was based upon San Francisco's Mission Dolores (founded in 1776 by Father Palou), the entrance to another copied from the San Gabriel Mission in Los Angeles. The plaza between the two was the paddock, the back wall buttressed like that of the San Gabriel Mission. They built the clubhouse to look like the Mission San Jose de Aguayo. The saddling shed was eventually overgrown with ivy.

Opening day, July 3, 1937, Crosby stood at the turnstiles taking tickets with a pipe between his teeth and a yachting cap jauntily perched atop his head.

He changed his clothes for the infield opening ceremony to a summery blue blazer, white slacks, and a boater.

The first post time was delayed, William Murray wrote. "The special train that the Santa Fe Railroad had dispatched, loaded with plungers from L.A., was late. When it finally appeared, through a gap in the hills just north of the track, everybody cheered. Cheering for the train, whether it was late or not, subsequently became a Del Mar tradition, which survived until the service was discontinued in the mid-Sixties."

At 2:24 on that first day, they were off. Fifteen thousand people saw a two-year-old gelding named High Strike get loose out front and run away with the race. The owner in the winner's circle was Mr. Crosby, a fact made only slightly less suspicious by the fact that High Strike went on to win four stakes races at Del Mar that year and the next.

The following day, eighteen thousand people showed up, cheered for the train, and laid down a quarter of a million dollars in bets. Things were looking good.

Charlie Wittingham, a legend of the California turf, came up from Tijuana to Del Mar. He was there every season from then on. He trained his horses in the surf, saying the salt water was good for them. Noble Threewit was there at the start and still trains as of this writing.

It was a relaxed haven, a horseman's paradise. The purses were small, but the weather was wonderful. Attendance was sometimes short—crowds that first year averaged just 4,654 daily over the 22-day meet—but they loved racing. Del Mar became—to pinch a phrase from William Murray, as he pinched it from a punter he knows—"a veritable Southland Saratoga."

It quickly established itself as a Hollywood playground. Stars of the screen roamed the clubhouse in those first years: Dorothy Lamour, W. C. Fields, Paulette Goddard, Edgar Bergen, June Haver, Ann Miller, Don Ameche, Ava Gardner, Red Skelton. Hoagie Carmichael played the parties.

Betty Grable and her bandleader husband Harry James were regulars. They owned and bred horses that ran at Del Mar. A plaque dedicated to her at the track reads: "Betty, you were as uplifting here as you were on the screen, and your spirit will live on these premises forever!"

Not all of the excitement was stardust. The racing was hot too. On August 12, 1938, Seabiscuit, owned by Charles Howard, met South American import Ligaroti, owned by Bing Crosby and Howard's son Lin, in a match race which drew twenty thousand people. The spectators were there for sport: there was no betting on this exhibition race. At least one mammoth side bet was laid down, though. The principals plunged, Charles Howard putting up fifteen thousand against his son's five grand that the Biscuit would take the race. Crosby and O'Brien stood at the mike, heading the radio broadcast of the race.

George Woolf, up on Seabiscuit, and Noel Richardson beat the hell out of each other on the stretch. Seabiscuit had led most of the way, but Ligaroti had come up on him in the last furlongs of the race. The jockeys punched, kicked, and whipped at each other. Richardson locked his leg around Woolf's. The stewards wanted them both banned for a year. But the order of finish stood. It was Seabiscuit by a nose. He'd run the track record for a mile and an eighth.

During the war, the track was dark, but in 1945 when it re-opened on August 15, 20,324 people showed up and passed $958,476 through the betting windows.

Success continued, and by 1989, Del Mar was the leading track in the country with a daily handle averaging over $7.5 million. Attendance was up, the area had been growing, and the old track was falling apart. The ivy was more structurally sound than the paddock building it supported, the joists of the grandstand were rotten. In 1991 a three-year renovation project began.

I never saw the old Del Mar, but I can say that the track to-day has all the character lauded in the original. The Del Mar Thoroughbred Club, a consortium made up mostly of horse-men, has managed the track since 1970, and their mission has been largely to maintain the spirit of the place. Don Smith once observed that the DMTC was going to "try to run this place for fun's sake," and that spirit lives on. The current president Joe Harper has said: "That's right. It's hard work having fun, too. You know what they say: Nobody is in a hurry here except the horses. We try to keep it that way. Every year I tell everybody, the staff, all of the people here, we're going to have a party for forty-three days, that's it. I've been going to the Oscars for fif-teen years, and opening day at Del Mar is a better party."

The racing has surely kept up its end of the deal. There have been some hilarious throwaway moments, such as when the spectator Russell Caputo jumped the rail and joined the race on foot (jockey Chris McCarron checked the favorite Sea of Serenity and avoided a collision), or when the jockey Francisco Mena's pants flew apart coming onto the stretch.

In 1996, Del Mar's new grandstand, with its double bell tower behind the tall palms, hosted its biggest crowd ever. The great Cigar drew 44,181 to watch the Pacific Classic. He had won sixteen races in a row, tying Citation for the record.

IT IS generally thought that the 1990s were not so good to horse racing—interest was supposed to be waning. I doubt this is true. Racetrack people are always grousing about the state of the sport. If you saw five thousand people at a physical plant built to support a hundred thousand—as you would see on most Wednesdays at Belmont—things might look pretty grim to you too. The fact is that many records were set in the early nineties. Keeneland had its highest average attendance for the fall meet in 1992; in 1994, Gulfstream handled more money than had ever been handled in Florida. In-state wagering at Pimlico was record-breaking in 1990 and again in 1994.

Del Mar's expansion wasn't due to an absence of interest in the track: you get the drift.

Yet the common suspicion was then—as it is now—that racing was on the decline.

For one thing, the track was no longer the only game in town. Lotteries had grown virtually ubiquitous; casinos were more and more common. (Why anyone would equate shoving money into a slot machine with horse racing is beyond me, but people seem to think there's some correlation.) It used to be that if you wanted some action, you had to head to the track. But the expansion of gambling possibilities was hitting its stride in the late eighties. By the nineties, racetrack officials must have felt as if they'd missed the riverboat.

There is also a prevalent suspicion that a huge chunk of the racing fan base is dead or must die soon. The railbird is perceived as endangered. You know them if you've ever been near a track, a jai alai game, a dog track, an OTB, or the Rascal House Delicatessen in Miami. They're at casinos and harness races too. They are old men in hats, smoking cigars. There are a hundred variations of railbird, from the Cadillac drivers to the bus riders, but they are of the same species, and they can't hang on forever.

Much has been written about these guys since they started being a suitable subject back in Damon Runyon's day. The problem is, of course, that I am not talking about the same type that Runyon knew; I am talking, literally, about the same guys. I saw Frankie the Horse just last week—he ain't looking so hot.

The racing world suspects that upon their demise the railbirds will not be replaced, and I think this suspicion really took hold in the late eighties and early nineties. But I don't think it's based in reality; I don't think we'll see the end of the show bet plunge. There are, after all, enough people out there to notice that these guys are passing. I'm out there, and for decades I plan to be smoking cigars, wearing hats, and betting like my grandfather.

I have come to believe that the misgivings about the future or the state of racing come not in fact from attendance size, handle numbers, or the imminent demise of the railbird. Del Mar, after all, is doing very well. The misgivings come, rather, from a lack of attention, a lack of buzz for all but a few races. Racing articles are not prominent on the sports pages of most newspapers. I'm lucky, there, in that the *New York Sun* gives me very good placement in their pages. I walk by the newsstand in the spring and see that my article about Derby Preps has a front-page header. Not so with other newspapers, bent on their relentless coverage of football, baseball, and basketball.

What team sports have, of course, that horse racing does not, is loyalty. As I've said, the only thing that makes for continuing affection at the track is a good overlay. Loyalty is hard to come by—just ask the jockeys who are getting hollered at every day around the country: "Yeah, thanks a lot, Tyler! Ya bum. What the hell are you doing out there? You didn't see the quarter pole or what?"

The Hogettes—the handful of Washington Redskins fans who costume themselves in flowered dresses, Mardi Gras beads, and floppy hats—aren't driven by an appreciation of the abstract qualities of the pro football. They're on hand to root for the Redskins. They have been driven mad with the sense that the Redskins are their team. The Redskins represent Good, and Dallas represents Evil, and when they war it's as if the fate of the nation were on the line.

Team loyalty is like being married for four decades to one woman whom you love very much. (Free agency confuses this issue, making the woman little more than a color combination and a logo, but let's leave that out of it.) Horse racing is more like dating. You spend a lot of time searching for the date. You find her, you go out with her, and most of the time the date is pretty exciting at some point (when it turns out that you and she both enjoy old-school red-sauce Italian food, or when the horse with your money on his nose gets up in front around the clubhouse turn). But it usually ends in disappointment (when you find out that you have absolutely nothing else in common, or that same little rabbit who was trying to run away with the race shows his true colors and sinks like a stone to stumble across the wire dead last). So you go back to the *Form*, and try to find another date.

Football, baseball, and basketball use team loyalty to build a church that you can join and believe in. Lucky for that church, the services are perfectly suitable for television. It is a single drama, in four or nine or two acts, with lots of time out for the advertisement of electric shavers, beer, and cars.

The only way to get that kind of loyalty at the racetrack is to march out a hero. More than anything, that was racing's problem in the early nineties. The eighties were a bit of a drought when it came to heroic racehorses. Sunday Silence versus Easy Goer was a good rivalry, but a far cry from Alydar versus Affirmed. The seventies had seen Secretariat, Ruffian, Spectacular Bid, Seattle Slew—every time you turned around there was another Big Horse. In the eighties, for whatever reason, the horses weren't there. Go for Wand was looking like the real thing, and then in 1990 she broke down, on national television, flailing around on the track at Belmont, in obvious pain, terrified, her hoof dangling gruesomely at the end of her leg.

That, more than anything, was why people sensed that racing was not doing so well. There were no heroes, and when one came along, she died horribly in front of millions of television viewers.

Enter Cigar. In 1994 trainer Bill Mott moved his horse off the turf and tried him on the dirt track. Cigar started to win. Then he really started to win.

No question but that Cigar was not a racehorse of the caliber of Secretariat, Citation, or Man o' War. Many believe he was not as good as Spectacular Bid or Affirmed. But it cannot be argued that at the end of his fourth year he started to run.

An allowance at Aqueduct came first. It was a race over a mile on the dirt, and he took it by eight lengths. Bill Mott was so impressed that he shot Cigar right up into graded stakes company, and in November he ran the NYRA Mile, a grade-one stakes race, also at Aqueduct, and took it by seven lengths. At the beginning of his fourth season, he had looked like a reasonable colt, a plodder. Certainly he'd earn his hay but one didn't expect much more. He ended that season looking like a potential champion. He was off to Florida for a little rest, and when he came back to the track, he blew the doors off the place.

He started out with a 1-1/16 mile allowance at Gulfstream, and took it by two lengths. He stepped right back up into graded-stakes company and conquered all comers. He ran a race a month, all of them with Jerry Bailey up in the irons, and he won them all: the Donn, the Gulfstream Park, the Oaklawn Park, and the Woodward Handicaps; the Pimlico Special, the Mass Cap, the Hollywood Gold Cup, and the Jockey Club Gold Cup. As a five-year-old he was nine for nine going into the Breeders' Cup Classic, and his most impressive showing, his biggest race, was still to come.

The Classic was run at Belmont on October 18, one year since Cigar had begun his streak. He had the very difficult tenth slot: the turn comes up very quickly at Belmont over a mile and a quarter, and it's easy to get shuffled around if you're way out off the inner rail. To make matters worse, the track was soup. It had been raining steadily. The mud was deep.

Star Standard got out front, followed closely by Cigar and and L'Carriere. The horses were handling the track badly. Their strides were all wrong. They were sliding around. The reins were loose at the horses' necks. These horses didn't want to go, they didn't want to be on this surface. It's one of those racing situations usually summed up in after race interviews with the phrase "didn't handle the track." That can't give the sense of it. It's a sliding, scrambling, muddy mess, clods of dirt and splashes of muddy water flying through the air. Things were not looking good.

Cigar didn't seem to notice, though. Jay Hovdey wrote of the race: "Even if their horses were handling the mud, one look at Bailey and their hearts sank. As Star Standard led the field down the backstretch and into the distant turn, Cigar was waging a war of isometric aggression with his jockey. It was Bailey's plan to wait as long as he could to give Cigar free rein. On this day, Cigar wanted to fly like the wind from the moment he left the starting gate."

So Bailey rode the race with his feet out in front of him, leaning back hard, pulling Cigar in as long as he could. It started to hurt. He was losing the battle. He needed Cigar to save some gas for the home stretch, but Cigar was arching his neck, pulling him forward: he wanted to run.

It was early for Cigar's move. Cigar's race was run on the stretch. Still, at the top of the turn Bailey started to let him out. It was as if the horse had been shot out of a cannon. Tom Durkin, the announcer, was obviously caught off guard. He's saying, "Three furlongs to go," and he doesn't even finish the word "go." It's more like "Three furlongs to g—CIGAR!"

"Cigar makes his move, and he sweeps to the lead with a dramatic rush with three furlongs to go and Jerry Bailey turns him loose."

Bailey checked over his left shoulder, where Unaccounted For and L'Carriere were behind and inside of him, and guided Cigar, who had just dashed through the mud and eaten the best horses in the world for lunch, down to the inside.

Durkin cried: "A quarter of a mile between Cigar and a perfect season."

Bailey switched his whip to his right hand and tapped Cigar on the flank, Cigar opened up. Bailey has said before that Cigar never stretched out, never got his belly down the way other horses settle in for their run. He may not have had a typical style when he reached the peak of his run, but you could tell as he hit the stretch that he was wide open. You could also tell he was going to win.

The crowd went insane. The roar, even on little media clips that I've downloaded, is akin to what I imagine it would be like to stand on the deck of an aircraft carrier.

Cigar opened up two and a half lengths. Bailey tucked his stick away and settled in. The horses behind Bailey and Cigar were in another race at this point, the race for second place.

Durkin's call of the finish is perfect: "And here he is! The UNCONQUERABLE, INVINCIBLE, UNBEATABLE CIGAR!"

His twelfth win in a row had been the fastest Breeders' Cup Classic ever run, and he'd done it over a muddy track that left most of the horses scrambling to get around the course at all.

Cigar rolled into his sixth year, which would make him the richest horse in history, like a locomotive. He went back and won the Donn again, then traveled to Dubai to win the first running of racing's richest, craziest race, the Dubai World Cup. In Massachusetts, for his second Mass Cap in a row, he was treated like royalty. In Chicago at Arlington, he took his sixteenth win in a row. He was tied with the great Citation for consecutive victories.

CIGAR'S ATTEMPT to break the record would take him to Del Mar for the 1996 Pacific Classic.

Horse racing was surely receiving all the attention it could handle by this point. The crowds when Cigar raced were capacity. He had come to be known as "America's Horse." The headlines were constant, and very much of a theme: TRAINERS LOOK TO STUB CIGAR; NOTHING LIKE AN AFTER-WINNER CIGAR (whatever that means); IN N.Y. FINALE FOES PUFF UP CIGAR, etc. I think a good bit of his fame might have come from how useful Cigar is as a headline—newspaper men love that stuff.

The Pacific Classic was to be huge. Dick Jerardi wrote in the *Philadelphia Daily News* that when "a parking lot attendant was asked what would be a good time to arrive to beat the [Saturday] crowds, he said: 'Friday.'" Jerardi's piece is a knockout, a great example of an article written before the big day.

Now, it's Del Mar, a track from another time and another place, a time when racing was king, a place where only racing matters.

Perhaps 100,000 eyes will see Cigar in the flesh today, millions more on television.

Cigar is America's horse and more.

"He's really everybody's horse," Bill Mott said.

Everybody awaits racing history. Everybody awaits Cigar.

It was typically sunny that Saturday. A real California paradise—the grandstand, the paddock, the apron, the boxes, the whole new Del Mar was packed with laid-back racing fans. They were enjoying their Del Margaritas while they indeed awaited Cigar. His name went up in a cry as Bailey leapt to his perch in the paddock.

The other horses were mostly ignored. Also in the paddock was Dramatic Gold, who had run against Cigar in Chicago, and Tinners Way, here to attempt a third Pacific Classic victory in as many years. They had both run against Cigar and lost. Richard Mandella, a California staple, and an excellent trainer, had two entries. Both were quick horses, one of them named Siphon and the other Dare and Go. Mandella had told the press that he would let Siphon go ahead and get loose, but that

you could rate Dare and Go, and he had told jockey Alex Solis to try to hold him off the pace and preserve his energy.

Bailey and Mott didn't seem worried about it. They had
the best horse in the race, by far. Cigar had beaten the other
horses, Dare and Go hadn't posted an important win in a year
and a half. Siphon was a rabbit; he wasn't going to run away
with a 1-1/4 mile race in front of Cigar. But he was going to try.

Some 44,000 fans cheered as the gates clanged open. It
wasn't the roar of the Eastern crowds. It was a more relaxed
California cheer. Cigar was going off the shortest-priced favorite ever entered in the Pacific Classic. He was 1-10.

As expected, Siphon shot out of the gate, gunning hard for
the lead. Bailey urged Cigar up there with him.

Siphon had won the Hollywood Gold Cup with a classic
front-runner strategy: he had set a false pace. Bailey was worried he might do it again, just sit out front, running slightly off
his best, saving it for the end, and then he'd turn it on. It is
very hard to catch a horse that's in front of you, especially after running one and a quarter miles, especially if that horse has
something left.

Bailey and Mott had talked about it and decided not to let
Siphon get away. They took the far turn like that, Siphon on
the lead, Bailey keeping him in his sights. Cigar wasn't pulling
as hard as he usually did, but Bailey wasn't worried about it.

Siphon and Cigar hit the backstretch out front. They'd run
the first quarter in a speedy twenty-three seconds.

Now Corey Nakatani brought Dramatic Gold up from
the field and into contention. He had been told to stay
within three lengths of the leader. The pace accelerated. Dra-

matic Gold was pressuring Cigar, and Cigar was pressuring Siphon, and the speed with which these horses were flying down the backstretch was now verging on suicidal. At the half, they clicked 45-4/5: the second quarter had gone two clicks faster than the first. Dramatic Gold was on the outside; Bailey was afraid he'd get boxed in. He had to stay a little ahead of Dramatic Gold, he figured, and that meant letting Cigar out to run. Siphon was still out front. The three were still tearing along.

When they came to the mile marker with only a quarter left to run, they were clocked at 133-3/5, only 2/5 of a second off of the track record for a mile. But this wasn't a mile race. They had another two furlongs to run.

Then the pressure valve released. Dramatic Gold caved in, exhausted. Nakatani had put him up in the race and he'd changed the running, but he wasn't going to make it.

Cigar ranged up on Siphon. Siphon had carried the lead through a blistering nine furlongs. When he caught sight of the big bay at his throatlatch, he caved.

Suddenly things looked all right. Cigar had the lead. He was running good around the turn. Bailey didn't have his stick out. Things were good. He was going to the stretch, a mere three furlongs away from history. Cigar was thirty-six seconds away from becoming the horse with the longest winning streak ever recorded. Cigar was going to make it.

But now Dare and Go, Mandella's other horse, started gaining. At first, perhaps, close watchers of the race believed he was only making up ground on tired horses. Siphon was dragging his feet, Dramatic Gold was dead on his shoes. There weren't many horses in the race for real anymore. Maybe Dare and Go wasn't making a move so much as he was simply not giving up. Maybe he was just passing the tired ones.

Wishful thinking. Alex Solis dug into Dare and Go as they hit the stretch.

Bailey put the stick to Cigar.

Dare and Go was out in the middle of the track, running wide, full of momentum. He was daring, all right, and he was going too. Solis was driving him hard.

Cigar gave it a shot. He tried to join the fight. But he had nothing left. He'd been wrecked by the pace. There was nothing in the tank.

Dare and Go got out front. Solis was pushing him. You don't get by a horse like Cigar and stop riding. Solis wanted daylight, and he got it. When they shot under the wire, Dare and Go was out front by three and a half lengths.

Bailey folded his hands on Cigar's withers. There was nothing coming at them. The horses up the track were struggling to finish at all. The streak was over.

Jim Murray wrote: "So Citation got a dead heat. Cigar couldn't beat him on the stretch."

Bailey thought Nakatani had rammed Dramatic Gold down his throat. "I would have been fine with what I was doing had Nakatani not had it in his mind to bury Cigar one way or another. He made the statement on a radio show that his job was to bury the favorite."

Nakatani viewed it differently. Bailey "can be as ticked off as he wants," Nakatani said. "I go out there trying to win. Because of the fact that Jerry rode a bad race, he's going to try to take it out on somebody else. I'm trying to beat the favorite every time I go out there. If you're on a 4-to-5 shot, especially in California, there are five guys out to get you. Jerry's a great rider, and he's got to realize that in big races, people are going to be trying to beat him."

Before the race, someone had asked Richard Mandella how he'd feel if he beat Cigar. "I'd feel terrible," he said, "for about a second."

"It was pure fun," he was later quoted as saying, "one of the high points of my racing career. One thing that racing proved that day is nobody gives anything away. You have to show up and run your horse."

The headlines read: STREAK TURNS TO ASHES; IN A PUFF OF SMOKE, CIGAR'S BID FOR 17 ENDS ON A DARE; CLOSE, BUT NO CIGAR.

CIGAR had been highly anticipated as a stallion. Coolmore Stud Farm had bought a three-quarter share in him from Allen Paulson, and his fee of $75,000 was the highest of any rookie stallion that year.

It didn't take all that long until the Italian insurance company Assicurazioni Generali found themselves the new owners of a $25 million retired racehorse that shot blanks. There will be no little Cigars, no Cigarillos proudly standing in the winner's circle. Eventually Cigar was sent to the Kentucky Horse Park. He's been racing up and down the paddock fence, and accepting visitors, ever since. I saw him last summer, nodding off in the straw, as far from the door as he could get. He hardly looked like the Big Horse. He wasn't tightly wound, or jumpy. He could have been just another horse on another farm but for his nameplate on the bridle. There he was: CIGAR.

9

Racing's Greatest Day, New and Improved

On November 10, 1984, Hollywood Park was glistening—freshly polished and newly improved. Led by Marje Everett, park officials had pulled out all the stops. They had built a new thirty-million-dollar Pavilion of the Stars, with forty swank suites and a hundred boxes. They had painted the walls of the grandstand orange and white, prompting George Vecsey of the *New York Times* to write that they'd made "the old grandstand glisten like the world's biggest root-beer stand." "Racing's Greatest Day" was painted on a brick wall in the infield. Six statues of rearing horses stood by the entrance. A legion of reporters and a crowd of 64,254 had gathered to watch an astonishingly good group of horses run in the richest program of racing ever staged. At the inaugural Breeders' Cup, no one had an idea what to expect.

THROUGHOUT these pages, two types of events are chronicled. The first is the dream of a new track, a better place for racing. Usually this is the dream of one man with a love of the sport and a desire to spend a lot of money to do it better than it had been done before.

This tradition goes way back. In 1711, Queen Anne was taking a carriage ride through the forest and saw a piece of ground she fancied for racing. She bought it for £558, had it fixed up, and began the Royal Ascot Festival. King George neglected it, but racing returned to Ascot in 1720, and it's been going ever since. Today Ascot is manicured horse heaven.

The second kind of event has more to do with racing's expansion, decentralization, and modernization. When John Henry won the inaugural Arlington Million he ushered in a new era of racing. Purses were fatter, and the big racing days had more to do with a nationwide competition for those purses than with the long-standing traditions of horsemen.

In the early 1980s, Kentucky breeder John Gaines had an idea. Instead of looking out at his pastures and dreaming of building the best track anyone had ever seen, Gaines cooked up a ten-million-dollar day of racing. The sprinters, the milers, the juveniles, the turf horses—each would have a race of their own. All the divisions would be represented. Topping it off, the best horses in the country would run in the three-year-old-and-up Classic. It's simple, he thought: why don't we do it all at once? And why don't we move the show like a traveling circus? It would happen at a different venue each year. John Gaines had boiled racing down to four hours on television and named it "The Breeders' Cup."

His idea would disrupt what had been a predictable progression from Florida through the Triple Crown and the classic races in Kentucky, Baltimore, and New York, then up to Saratoga, then back again to Belmont. Autumn races like the Jockey Club Gold Cup and the Champagne had traditions behind them. Belmont had long decided the divisional champions at its fall meet. It goes without saying that racing had long had its greatest day on the first Saturday in May. The crowd at Hollywood Park would not be slurring through the verses of "My Old Kentucky Home."

It was a fresh idea, but it was a natural. It fit with the expansion and decentralization that had been happening in racing, and it suited the new type of trainer that had emerged on the scene.

In 1978, D. Wayne Lukas moved from a successful decade training quarter horses and began what would be a stellar career training thoroughbreds. He saw plenty of good races across the country in which he could run horses. Trainers passed up good races because they were too far away. Rare was the horse that would ship to run in a stakes race. It had been done, of course. Seabiscuit ran all over the country, and Jim Dandy shipped in to run in his Travers. But these were exceptions. Mostly, trainers ran at their own tracks. They'd ship for the Derby, they'd ship for the Travers, but most of their stable ran within a few hundred yards of the barn.

Lukas decided not to stick to one track. He wouldn't be just a California trainer. Why run only in reasonable allowance races, waiting for the big one? He began shipping horses everywhere, to stakes races all over the country. He worked like a demon and had a huge staff. He was accused of not being a horseman, of being rather a businessman. For almost a decade, 1983 to 1992, he was racing's leading earner.

Lukas ran a large stable of expensive horses, and his barn always looked the part: flowers, freshly mown grass, and spotless surfaces. When an owner takes a trip to one of Lukas's barns he does not see towels drying on a worn out string in front of his $750,000 baby. Jack Van Berg, too, deserves credit for instituting this new kind of training. Regardless of who started it, the model has been picked up and copied. There are those who would point out that Steve Asmussen's total victories per year have nothing to do with the records of trainers like Sunny Jim and Whittingham, because Asmussen runs about four hundred horses—ten times the number found in those old trainers' barns. Others would point out that Asmussen, Todd Pletcher, and other trainers with huge outfits that spread across the nation can't possibly be training those horses themselves. However one feels about it, super trainers have become some of the most important figures in the game today.

They chase purses like the one offered in the Breeders' Cup Classic, which would be run at Hollywood Park over a mile and a quarter for three million dollars.

THE CLASSIC was the last race. The day had been exciting. A mare named Princess Rooney had romped in the Distaff. Royal Heroine, the only filly in the field, had set a track record in the Mile. But the best race of all, without question, was still to come. The next race would turn the Classic into just that—an immediate classic.

The paddock at Hollywood Park is planted with palms and bizarre Dr. Seuss trees that are trimmed into topiary shapes like abstract representations of well-groomed poodles. Out there that afternoon, under the façade of the grandstand covered with plaques painted after the silks of stables that have run there, no one was looking at Wild Again, trained by Vincent Timphony. Timphony was not a super trainer. "I'm a man with one good horse," he said. And that horse hadn't even been nominated for the Breeders' Cup: his owners had coughed up $360,000 to send him to the gate. That's a very big gamble.

"He deserved to be here 100 percent because we couldn't pass on a $3 million race when he had a chance of winning," Timphony told the press. He didn't look like he had a chance of winning.

As a three-year-old in 1983, Wild Again had bone chips, had started only once, and had finished out of the money.

At four he was having his best year and picking up some stakes purses. He won in New Orleans and at Oaklawn. He won the Meadowlands Cup, a Grade One race. But the Classic would be a tough group of horses, classic winners and champions. Wild Again hadn't run in a field like this.

Slew o' Gold was the big horse. He'd been the three-year-old of the year in 1983. He'd taken a long time off and come back to romp away seven and a half lengths ahead at Belmont Park. They hadn't even expected him to win it; he hadn't raced in nine months. Mickey Taylor, his owner, told Steve Crist, writing for the *New York Times*, "You can't win them all." A few minutes later, after Slew o' Gold had burned through the mile in 1:34-2/5, obliterating the field, Taylor exulted: "Maybe we *can* win them all."

That was the plan, and that was what the world expected. Slew o' Gold's schedule was designed to drop him into the gate on November 10, 1984, in the richest race ever run, the first Breeders' Cup Classic.

Andy Beyer wrote in the *Washington Post*: "Slew o' Gold has won all of his races this year with such authority that he might seem unbeatable. When co-owner Mickey Taylor talked the other day about his horse's prospects in Saturday's $3 million Breeders' Cup Classic, he sounded as if he thought the outcome was a foregone conclusion."

But as everyone knows, you've got to get around the track in front before they give you the trophy.

There was also the dazzlingly quick Precisionist. He had won the Hollywood Derby by ten lengths, out front the whole way. Andy Beyer wrote: "In the Del Mar Handicap, he set a seemingly suicidal pace—running the first half mile in 45 seconds flat—and still managed to win in brilliant time. Then he went to the $500,000 Super Derby at Louisiana Downs, controlled the pace, opened a three-length lead turning for home and was caught at the wire by Gate Dancer. The two horses broke the track record for 1-1/4 miles by more than a second."

Most people were looking at Gate Dancer. Not only had he broken a track record in Louisiana, pulling Precisionist along with him, he had set a record at the Preakness too. Late in the season he was looking even better. He was growing up. The race was going to be fast, and Gate Dancer liked to close.

Mr. and Mrs. Cary Grant at Hollywood Park.

CALIFORNIA might not have needed a third track in the 1930s, but certain folks definitely wanted one. Chief among them was Jack L. Warner of Warner Bros. When Jack called and said you should think about buying stock in a racetrack, you bought it. Al Jolson, Walt Disney, Bing Crosby, Samuel Goldwyn, Ralph Bellamy, and Mervyn LeRoy were stockholders.

This was to be a movie track, not a cowboy track or a seaside resort. This track was wrapped up in a silver screen. This track was modern, Hollywood.

Actually, it was fifteen miles south of Hollywood, in Inglewood. The press office tried to say that the ocean breezes kept it cooler than the town. Biff Lowry wrote the book on Hollywood Park—literally, it's titled *Hollywood Park: From*

Seabiscuit to Pincay—and he tells a great story of the press tours at the opening.

After showing the newspapermen around, the principals announced it was time for the luncheon at Warner Bros. Al Kahn of the United Press piped up, "Wait a minute, you haven't shown us the press box yet."

Silence. "Oh, we're still working on that."

They'd forgotten it entirely. So they built it into the top row of the stands.

The "thrown together" press box turned out pretty well except for the fact that occupants of the front row were just a thick pane of glass away from members of the public . . . [who would] turn around and razz a turf-writing handicapper whose best bet had just finished out of the money as an odds-on favorite. Pedo Bernard, of *The Examiner*, and Paul Lowry, of *The Times*, took to putting up large 3-foot by 4-foot pieces of cardboard in front of them, which they took down when a race went off, and then would replace immediately after the horses hit the wire. "Keeps the glare out of my eyes while I'm working," explained Lowry.

A similar flub occurred with regard to the urinals in the jocks room—they were built too high. Boxes had to be constructed for the jocks to stand on. All of this provided entertainment over at Santa Anita, and proved to the competition that they had nothing to worry about.

After a fire in the fifties, the grandstand was rebuilt. Rebuilt Hollywood Park has a streamlined, tubular, pink-and-aqua mix of frivolity and practicality. It makes me think that just out of sight is a rotating glass case filled with cream pies. The whole facility is shiny clean and riotously colorful: turquoise, aqua, peachy pink, burgundy, the deep salmon of nova lox, striped poles, yellow stair rails, all with grey painted metal I-beams supporting the roof. Movie posters abound, and though they pay tribute to the very stars that once haunted the track, they now seem to contribute to the diner feel. Metal bar stools stand below fifties deco-style mirrored wall sconces. There is a hint of faded glamour everywhere, memories of a rosy past. This diner was once very popular, very glamorous, then it tanked, and now it's cool again, but they still have a bowl of powdery mints by the cash register. This was the writer Charles Bukowski's track. He wrote:

> The track had changed. Forty years ago there had been some joy out there, even among the losers. The bars had been packed. This was a different world. There was no money to blow to the sky, no to-hell-with-it money, no we'll-be-back-tomorrow money. This was the end of the world. Old clothing. Twisted and bitter faces. The rent money. The 5 dollars an hour money. The money of the unemployed, of the illegal immigrants. The money of the petty thieves, the burglars, the money of the disinherited. The air was dark. And the lines were long. They made the poor wait in long lines. The poor were used to long lines. And they stood in them to have their small dreams smashed.
>
> This was Hollywood Park, located in the black district, in the district of Central Americans and other minorities.

One of the bizarre aspects of horse racing is that it is both agricultural and urban. A track is at once a farm and an arena. On every backside are chickens running around, goats on tethers, and tan men in cowboy boots cooking hamburgers on a grill with a beer in hand and the radio on. Every backside has tractors and hay bales and manure pits. In the grandstand, by contrast, are hot-dog vendors, elevators, newspapers, tablecloths, wineglasses, and all manner of very unagricultural items.

Nowhere is this confluence and contrast more vivid than at Hollywood Park. This must be due, at least in part, to the track's location in Inglewood. Inglewood is a gritty, urban city, mostly black and Hispanic, in Los Angeles County. Other tracks are hemmed in by their cities. Other tracks require that their patrons drive through rough-edged cityscapes to gain entrance. Nowhere I've been does the city at the edge of the track feel so at hand.

THE BUGLER blew the call to the post for the biggest race of the day, and the horses glided out on to the track. Slew o' Gold walked to the gate almost an even-money favorite. Gate Dancer was 7-1. Precisionist, the speedy wire-to-wire runner, was 15-1. The longest shot on the board was Wild Again.

When the gates flew open, the longest shot popped out like he'd been shocked. He got up in the race, pushing for the lead immediately. But it was Precisionist in front for the first quarter mile. He held it by only a head. Slew o' Gold had been entered with another horse, a rabbit used to set a brisk early pace and arrange the race for the big closer. His name was Mugatea, and he was right up there, breathing down Precisionist's neck, pushing him on. Wild Again was third, only a head behind Mugatea.

They covered the first quarter mile in 22-3/5, blazing fast for a race this long. The three leaders were six lengths ahead of the pack. The big horses were saving their strength among the plodding middle pack.

By the half-mile, Precisionist had sunk to third, and the already fading Mugatea was still second. Around the clubhouse turn, Mugatea lugged out. He wasn't running well. He'd be fifth by the three-quarter, dropping like a stone. By the time they made their way past the newly improved grandstand, the Pavilion of Stars, and all the swells in the box seats, Wild Again had pushed his way to the front.

MARJE EVERETT brought the Breeders' Cup to Hollywood Park in 1984. The road that brought Marje to Hollypark in 1971 was circuitous. Her grandfather was Jacob Lindheimer, a key figure in the early building of the Chicago Democratic political machine. Ben Lindheimer, Marje's father, worked in that machine to get Henry Horner elected governor in 1932. For his efforts, Ben was appointed chairman of the commerce commission—but he wanted to own racetracks. Other people already owned the Chicago racetracks, of course.

In 1933, Ben Lindheimer set up the Illinois Racing Commission and pushed through a law that "persons engaged in illegal business, bookmakers, and any other type of undesirables" could not own or run a racetrack.

At the time Jack Lynch owned most of Washington Park. Lynch had gotten very rich owning 40 percent of the wire service called the General News Bureau. He was fighting Moses Annenberg to keep his chunk of the wires, because Annenberg wanted the whole thing. Although he was manager of General News, Annenberg founded a rival, the Nationwide News Service, to drive General News out of business.

Lynch sued.

Most of the "news" carried over the wire consisted of race results delivered to the first off-track betting parlors, known as handbooks. Annenberg's defense against Lynch's suit was that the wire service to handbooks was illegal; therefore the court had no jurisdiction.

Annenberg won, and Lynch was reminded of the racing commission's new rule that forbade persons engaged in illegal business to own or operate racetracks.

Lynch was over a barrel. He sold his shares in the Washington Park to Ben Lindheimer for three cents each.

Lindheimer quickly forgot whatever morality to which he had pretended and got down to the business of making money.

Bookies in Chicago paid track odds—that is, whatever the odds on the pari-mutuel board were, that's what bettors got. Suppose a bookie finds himself with a big bet that he might not be able to cover? Suppose he typically handles ten thousand dollars a day and some high roller has just dropped five thousand on a horse going off at 10-1? If the bookie loses that bet, he's out fifty thousand, which will likely drive him out of business immediately. One of the ways he can get around this is to pay into the pari-mutuel machines at the track and drive the odds down. In *The Politics of Prosecution*, Hank Messick wrote:

> The [horse] might go off at 10-1. If it lost, Lindheimer simply put the money in his pocket. If the horse won, he quickly dumped the money in the mutuel pool, and the *final* payoff odds flashed on the tote board would reflect the post-race bet and come down to perhaps 8 to 5, thus saving the bookie from financial disaster.

Messick estimates that Lindheimer handled a million dollars a week before the laws were tightened up in 1940. Ben must have made enough money by then; it was the same year he picked up the majority share of Arlington Park. In 1955 he bought Lincoln Fields and changed the name to Balmoral Park.

His loving adopted daughter, Marjorie, was a great fan of horses and the track. She was in the mix from the start. She was fourteen when Ben acquired Washington Park, and by 1940 Marje was officially his assistant. She knew about the box of cash in the office for greasing palms and making gifts. She knew about the tricks with bookie money. She knew the whole world of racing.

Eventually she inherited all the tracks from her father. Her headquarters were at Arlington. She paved most of it, all but eradicating the color green, which she didn't like. She converted the Post and Paddock Club (which would later be the spark of the great fire) into a private residence. She cut down as many trees as she could. Her attempts to control Chicago racing were brazen, gutsy, and slightly nuts. In 1967 the swirl of debt and corporations proved unmanageable, and Marje made a deal with Gulf and Western.

It made her rich. She sold to the conglomerate for $21,534,500 and stayed on as CEO at a salary of $50,000. She got to keep her house at Arlington.

It wouldn't last. She was fired in 1970. She sued, claiming fraud, conspiracy, and SEC violations.

In June 1971 the suits were settled, and Marje found herself the new owner of a majority stake in another racetrack in another part of the country. That's how Marje moved to Los Angeles and how she came to Hollywood Park. Oddly enough, it worked out for her. She had married a major shareholder of the track years before.

THE HORSES had covered the half-mile in 45-1/5. No one watching the race would have thought that the 31-1 shot on the lead was going to stick this race out. The times were too fast. He was just running with the rabbits, hoping to steal something. Maybe the rallies would be few enough to allow him to grab a little of the money. Third place in a stakes race ain't so bad. In this, the most expensive race ever run, third place was worth $324,000. You've got to buy the hay. Even fourth place, which was worth $210,000, would recoup some of the $360,000 that the owners laid down to put Wild Again in the gate.

But up in the irons on Wild Again was Pat Day, who does not typically run horses out front like that. He's Patient Pat.

He's a waiter and a closer. He rates. He holds the horse back. Rating a pace in a forty-five-second half-mile? Apparently so.

At the three-quarter pole, Slew o' Gold came up into the game. He had not been hurried. His race had been slow and settled-in, and now he ranged up on the leaders, looking for the entire world like he was about to take control.

At a mile, Precisionist was done. He was all out of gas. The speed was failing. The closers were coming. The race was unfolding as it should, just as you'd expect a mile and a quarter to be run. With one exception: Wild Again was still in the race.

IN 1948, Biff Lowry was a college kid working in the publicity office of Hollywood Park when Webb Everett, the racing secretary at Santa Anita, walked in. An owner named A. A. Hirschberg followed him in. Hirschberg owned a lot of horses, a chain of Pig 'n' Whistle restaurants, and the House of Murphy restaurant. He also owned a hefty chunk of Hollywood Park.

Webb Everett asked Lowry if he could type a check. Biff Lowry wrote about the scene years later: "The kid"—that being Lowry; he saved his identity in the story for the punchline— "rolls Everett's check into the Underwood, and Webb directs him to make it out to A. A. Hirschberg. Then he says quietly, 'Type in this number.' The number is dutifully typed, both numerically and spelled out. The kid has never seen a check with so many zeros. . . . It takes awhile for the episode to sink in. After it does, the kid begins to wonder how in the world a working guy like Webb Everett—albeit a reasonably well-paid racing secretary, but nevertheless a second-level racing executive—can accumulate enough money to write a check as big as that one. He eventually poses the question to his father, who shrugs and says, 'Maybe it's someone else's money.'"

In 1957, Marje Lindheimer and Webb Everett were married.

In 1976, Whitney Tower in *Classic* magazine estimated that Marje Everett owned between 10 and 11 percent of the stock in Hollywood Park, four times as much as any other stockholder.

By all reports, Marje was calmer at Hollywood. She had been a terror—quick tempered and quick to fire people. She had run her house in the old Post and Paddock club at Arlington as Marje's Inn, with twenty-four-hour service and late-night poker games. But she'd also demanded that many of her friends travel to attend the funeral of her favorite dog. She was a tough cookie. Turnover was still high, but California softened her.

"We're spending $10 million in renovation," she told Whitney Tower. "$4 million on the backstretch alone."

Tower wrote:

> Marje probably always will be the subject of controversy, but there can be little doubt, too, that the Hollywood track is now the country's most progressive, both from the standpoint of management as well as in improved racing and benefits to horsemen. Part of the $4 million spent on the backstretch has gone into the construction—at $500,000 apiece—of four new 100-stall barns, complete with living quarters. There is also a 72-stall barn and plans for more on the way. On the

backstretch itself, there is a new track kitchen and rec hall with betting facilities and a wide porch from where the stable help can watch the afternoon racing.

Not only the backstretch got attention: "I want this place to be the best possible track for customers." Whitney Tower listed some of the foods that Marje made available toward this end: Chow Mein Burger, Hungarian Apple Strudel, Baked Viennese Gugelhopf, Onion Mustard Dog, Tortilla Chili Dog, Enchilada Plate, Fish Creole Jumbalaya, Baked Red Snapper à la Dyglere, Fish and Chips, German Chocolate Layer Cake.

Her program of improvement had paid off. She'd moved from Snapper à la Dyglere to the Pavilion of Stars, and in 1984 she was hosting the first Breeders' Cup, the most extravagant day of racing ever seen.

IN THE most expensive race ever run, Wild Again was sticking it out, digging deep, but Slew o' Gold, the heavy favorite, the champion three-year-old in a year that Wild Again hadn't even hit the board, was ranging up on him on the outside.

And here came Gate Dancer. Gate Dancer wore a ridiculous hat, with pockets that covered his ears and blinkers, but he could move. On the outside he came, wide around the whole turn, picking off horses one at a time.

Going into the stretch, a horse named Track Barron angled out hard—Gate Dancer just drifted right by him, cruising.

Down on the inside rail, Wild Again was showing astonishing game. Slew o' Gold was right there, looking like he should just blow by him, but somehow Patient Pat and Wild Again were holding him off. Slew o' Gold wasn't getting by.

With one furlong to go, Gate Dancer caught the two leaders. They were five lengths in front of the pack. They weren't five millimeters away from one another.

They hit the final yards of the race in a battle. Gate Dancer was running sloppily. Slew o' Gold and Wild Again brushed repeatedly. Gate Dancer lugged in and bumped Slew o' Gold hard. Slew o' Gold slammed into Wild Again.

Wild Again would not give up.

The three chugging thoroughbreds hit the wire almost together. It looked like Wild Again. The track announcer called "Wild Again! the upset winner here, but it really was a bit too close to call."

The confusion would last.

The steward's inquiry light flashed on almost immediately.

Who would be disqualified? It was so close, and there had been so much contact that a case could be made for the disqualification of any one of the three leaders.

"Up to the sixteenth pole," said steward Alfred Shelhamer, "there was incidental contact, not enough to warrant a disqualification. In the final sixteenth of a mile, something definitely happened."

It was in the final sixteenth that Gate Dancer had arrived on the scene. They didn't dress him up in that silly costume for nothing: he was an easily distracted horse. When he reached the leaders, he lost an incredible amount of momentum. It looked like he would rip right past them, but he just sat down next to them and lugged in.

People were milling about on the sidelines, waiting for the decision. This was national television. Something had to be done. Andy Beyer wrote:

> Over and over, the films showed the space separating the three horses growing tighter and tighter, until Slew o' Gold's jockey, Angel Cordero Jr., was squeezed back in the final yards. But Shelhamer told the audience, "Just watch the harrow marks."
>
> The tractors used for maintenance purposes leave lines on the racing strip, and by watching those lines it was possible to see that Wild Again was keeping a straight course. "You couldn't ask a rider to hold a horse any straighter," said former jockey Bill Hartack, now a patrol judge here.

They disqualified Gate Dancer. Slew o' Gold was second in the final race of his career. Wild Again had just paid back a $360,000 gamble, big time.

Pat Day has ridden in every Breeders' Cup since that first one, and is the only jockey to have done so. Every big-time jockey has a race that put him over the top, that made him a sought-after jock. For Pat Day, this had been it. He had rated a horse through blazing fractions, held off a rush from the biggest horse running, and held his line while being walloped in the final strides. "My single biggest victory was the very first Classic on Wild Again," he once observed. "That did more for my career than any other race."

10
It's Just One Furlong Away . . .

B y the time we got to Belmont on June 5, 2004, we had all gone around the bend. We were possessed. All wisdom was gone, all reason replaced by a mad enthusiasm for the high theater that Smarty Jones and Team Smarty had created. The horse was undefeated, the story was perfect.

Jockey Stewart Elliott is a survivor, a hard worker, a horseman. He had been cool under the spotlights when his reputation caught up with him (nothing, really—an assault charge he'd rather ignore than report to the stewards at Churchill Downs). He seemed unflappable in the saddle too. He was in the biggest races of his life, and he was keeping it together and doing his job. It's a job he loves. He'd quit and come back, and battled with weight, and alcohol. At a press conference following the win in the Kentucky Derby: "Why'd you come back to racing, Mr. Elliott?" asked a reporter.

"Racing is all I got. This is all I've wanted to do since I was a kid. It's all I've done. I don't have anything else. What else am I supposed to do?" Stewart Elliott does not see his life as a story, and his answer was too blunt to be useful. He'd dropped out of school to race horses and had never done anything else.

Pat and Roy Chapman, the elderly owners of Smarty Jones, had almost quit racing. Their trainer had been Bob Camac, who was murdered along with his wife, Maryann, by her son, Wade Russell. According to reports at the time, Camac suspected that his stepson had been cashing checks sent to the trainer by owners, and planned to confront him. On December 6, 2001, the Camacs were found dead of gunshot wounds on the back porch of their farmhouse in Oldman's Township, southern New Jersey. Their murder rocked the community of horsemen that race in Delaware and Philadelphia Parks.

The Chapmans were sad. Roy spends most of his time in a wheelchair, hooked up to an oxygen tank. (He is not without humor about this: "You can see what my problem is," I heard him say to reporters one day, laughing.) They sold most of their horses and pretty much quit the game. But they kept Smarty. Pat Chapman liked him. She had named him after her grandmother, after all. And anyway, he looked like he had something real.

So they moved their diminished stable to John Servis's barn. Servis had worked all his life in semi-obscurity, hitting the big time just once with a good stakes runner but never really going to The Show. Servis said he would never go to the Derby unless he could win it, so he raced plodders at Philadelphia Park. He is smart and humble.

Early in Smarty's training, they were schooling him at the gate—trying to coax one thousand pounds of high-strung muscle into a bizarre metal contraption—and the first thing Smarty Jones did was to almost kill himself when he reared up and knocked his head. Servis thought for sure the colt had done himself in. But he was alive, and they nursed him back to health. Now he had that little mark on his forehead—not a small star of white fur but a scar.

Servis must have known from the beginning. When Smarty Jones hit the track, Servis must have recognized that Smarty had the thing all horsemen wait for. John Servis had nursed back to health the Big Horse, the really, really Big Horse. He started sketching out the course. You can imagine Servis taking the Chapmans out to lunch, not quite able to believe what he is saying to them, nervous that he'll jinx it: "If he does well, if he doesn't get hurt, if he keeps running, we'll race him here and then here, and then Mr. and Mrs. Chapman, we'll be sitting in a box on the first Saturday in May."

Smarty Jones did keep running, and he didn't get hurt. All Smarty Jones could do was win.

Servis would bump him up, run him against stiffer competition, and he'd win again.

Come April 2004, the season of Derby Preps—what trainer Bob Baffert has referred to as "the balloon-busting time of year"—Smarty Jones was in the right spot. Saturday, April 10, was a big Derby Prep weekend. Three of the most important races leading to the Derby, the races that would decide who goes and at what odds, ran the same day: the Wood Memorial at Aqueduct, the Blue Grass Stakes at Keeneland, and out in Arkansas, at Oaklawn, the Arkansas Derby. Here's what I wrote in the paper that Friday:

At Oaklawn, on Saturday, it's all about the Grade II, 1-1/8 mile Arkansas Derby, and the Arkansas Derby is all about Smarty Jones.

The colt is undefeated in five starts, winning them by a combined 31-1/2 lengths. He keeps stepping up in class, and he keeps getting it done. It's conceivable that Smarty Jones will hit his ceiling down the road, but I don't see the horse that's going to beat him this weekend. If Smarty Jones wins, he'll be only the 18th horse to go to the Derby undefeated; five of those went on to win it.

And Monday:

The best story of the weekend, however, centers on the horse that will no doubt be this year's star: Smarty Jones. If you thought last year's Funny Cide story was sweet, this one's a humdinger. . . .

Smarty has stepped up in class each time out, and he's pulled a victory out of each one. In Arkansas, he was not set up well. He had the 11th post position, which won't look so bad come a Derby field of 20, but was tough enough on a muddy track. He jumped out of the gate and got in front with speedster Purge.

Their first quarter-mile was a full second faster than either had run at the Blue Grass or the Wood, and whereas The Cliff's Edge and Tapit both started their respective races far off the pace, Smarty Jones was never more than half a length off the lead in Arkansas. Smarty Jones has lived up to every race he's entered; he's got serious strength and real guts.

There were a few weeks left before we started pouring the juleps. Most of the time was spent racing those winners and a few others in imaginary Kentucky Derbies. From California came the gutsy Imperialism, an experienced runner in Kristin Mulhall's stable. The trainer was young, in her early twenties, and she rode him herself when he exercised. There was the speed flashing Lion Heart, a horse deserving his name. He ran out front, but on the stretch he wouldn't give up. He dug in like the stretch run was the Western Front, and he stuck. But The Cliff's Edge had caught him, because the closing move of The Cliff's Edge was second only to the closing move displayed by Tapit, who had won the Wood by closing like a slammed door after picking off the entire field one at a time in a determined drive to the wire. Then there was the shimmering, dappled, muscular Rock Hard Ten. He looked like a classic horse. He was giant, sturdy, and fast, though unmanageable. He'd lug all around on the stretch, he'd balk at the gate.

Rock Hard Ten was young and crazy, but generally, somehow, as we'd moved through the spring, these flighty two-year-olds had grown up. As we waited for the Derby, it seemed like we had a gate full of real racehorses. They'd never run the distance, and most of them had never run against one another, but they were looking more and more like a field worthy of the Run for the Roses.

At the 2004 Derby, the rain came in great sheets, turning the track into soup. Some ran for cover, others threw up makeshift tents. A family sat calmly under thirty yards of clear plastic, still sipping juleps and chatting while the water ran like a river at their feet.

Stewart Elliott was crossing his fingers, looking at the sky and saying, "Let it rain!"

I was under cover—barely—talking with some lucky friends who had grandstand seats in the first sheltered row. We stared in disbelief at the track: I swear it had currents, lunar tides. Big tractors were sealing it, pushing the dirt tighter with heavy drag plates.

"Will it be wet sloppy or wet fast?" asked one of my friends.

"Who knows?" I answered. "You could go bass fishing in there. All bets are off."

Of course, all bets weren't off. I'd laid mine hours before, and you can't walk up to the window and change your mind. There is no "act of God" clause in gambling.

Bang—eighteen horses hit the first stretch run in the ridiculous slop. It was a traffic jam. They all smashed together. Except for Lion Heart, who came away with a jump like a kangaroo and managed to get out front. Smarty Jones was crushed between horses, and if you watched carefully, you got the first clue as to why we all went crazy for Smarty Jones.

It's muddy, it's crowded, 100,000 people are screaming at the top of their lungs, and Smarty Jones gets crushed between two horses while trying to get up in the race before the turn. Elliott doesn't lose his cool. The horse doesn't lose his cool. They don't check. They don't balk.

Elliott engaged Smarty's incredible tactical speed and spurted him up past the traffic. By the time they were halfway through the first turn, Elliott had him in a good spot.

We all went nuts because Smarty didn't need excuses, and his connections didn't make them. After the race we heard that the morning-line favorite, The Cliff's Edge, lost his shoes. Michael Dickinson, trainer of Tapit (who I thought would win), said that things were "sticky." Song of the Sword kept getting "stuck on the ground," said his jockey Norberto Arroyo. Alex Solis, up on Master David, who finished twelfth, said, "He started slipping and sliding. He wasn't handling it."

But before the excuses were made, Lion Heart was running with the wind at his back. The call on the backstretch was: "Lion Heart throws down the gauntlet and opens up three . . . Smarty Jones is a stalking second as they approach the far turn."

Heading into that turn, Imperialism was fighting like a wolverine to get up into the running. Tapit had turned it on and was picking off horses by running up the outside. The Cliff's Edge had moved with him—there was plenty of action. The call doesn't even note that Stewart Elliott had spurred Smarty Jones, and that he was now breathing down Lion Heart's neck. But when they came around the turn, the track announcer Tom Durkin got it. The horses turned for home, "and undefeated Smarty Jones comes wide off the turn!" They hooked up at the top of the stretch. "Lion Heart is all heart! Smarty Jones is all out!" They were opening up on the field. "Those two, deadlocked at the eight pole! And Smarty Jones is roused to the lead by journeyman jockey Stewart Elliott! . . . And here is the first UNDEFEATED winner of the Kentucky Derby since Seattle Slew in 1977! Smarty Jones has done it!"

I saw on the replays that the camera cut to the the Chapmans' box, Roy standing, grinning from ear to ear, laughing with the oxygen tubes dangling from his nose. John Servis hug-

Smarty Jones gets his morning bath a few days before the Belmont Stakes.

ging him, a kid hanging off of John Servis's neck, all of them overjoyed, while Durkin announced, "What a day for Stewart Elliott, the thirty-nine-year-old journeyman jockey has just won the race of a lifetime!"

We all fell in love.

At the post-Derby press conference, a reporter asked if Smarty Jones could capture the imagination of America.

Stewart Elliott answered, "I think we just did."

It didn't stop there. The Preakness was a romp. On the Friday before the race I wrote: "The duel for second will be a brilliant battle between Lion Heart and the tenacious Rock Hard Ten. The duel for show could be a tooth-and-nail fight between Borrego and Imperialism. Smarty Jones, meanwhile, will pull away and win this one, too."

I was partially right. Lion Heart finally faded on the stretch and slipped back to fourth. Rock Hard Ten did finally rally, and got up to place. Imperialism didn't show up, but a horse named Eddington did. None of it mattered. Elliott let Mike Smith ride Lion Heart out front, shadowing the whole way around. When Elliott wanted it, he took it. At the top of the stretch, Smarty had opened up five lengths. At the wire he crashed home a whopping 11-1/2 lengths ahead of the field. It was the largest margin of victory ever run in the Preakness.

And it was a recipe for widespread insanity.

No matter how many times we'd seen this before—a horse with a chance at history—we all knew this was the one. 2004 was Smarty's Party. He was on the news, he was in the magazines, and he was all over the papers.

The pull from the front page of the *New York Sun* to my article in the sports section of May 17 read: "Why Smarty Jones Will Win the Triple Crown."

My lead: "Get ready: The show is coming to town. Barring a weather forecast that calls for earthquakes and a rain of frogs, the attendance at this year's Belmont Stakes, run June 5, should smash War Emblem's record draw. After a masterful win in the Derby, after tearing it up in the Preakness, Smarty Jones is coming to New York to win the Triple Crown."

It just got worse. Another headline: "Believe the Hype, Smarty Jones Looks Unbeatable."

Then, in the week before the race, in a masterful piece of marketing, the National Thoroughbred Racing Association held a press conference with the living connections of past Triple Crown winners. Ron Turcotte, who rode Secretariat to a thirty-one-length victory at the Belmont to win the Triple Crown, said he thought Smarty Jones was twenty-five-lengths better than any three-year-old running. "SMARTY WILL WIN BY 25 LENGTHS, TURCOTTE VOWS."

We never learn.

Certainly the world felt that when Spectacular Bid went into the gate in 1979 he was about to notch Triple Crown number twelve. A safety pin destroyed those dreams: it was lodged in his hoof.

Lots of folks thought War Emblem would do it. He looked like a Big Horse in 2002, when I was going to the track to watch him work out in the rain. The day of the Belmont Stakes, teenyboppers with stars painted on their faces had Go War Emblem stickers on the back pockets of their Capri jeans. The sun was shining; 103,222 people were there to see it happen. When they broke from the gate, Tom Durkin called, with surprise evident in his voice, ". . . and War Emblem's quest for the Triple Crown . . . he did not break alertly . . . War Emblem is OFF near the back of the pack."

We would have no idea, until we saw the photos, just how badly War Emblem had started. Both his knees had hit the ground right in front of the gate. It's amazing he ran that race with a rider.

It didn't stop there; you couldn't invent a worse race. War Emblem was up in it, and then the front-runners bottled him up on the backstretch. He pushed through an inviting opening on the rail coming around the backstretch, but he didn't have the mile and a half in him. Not after the stumble, not after being hemmed in like that. He was held hard on the backstretch, reined in. And then: "There's an inviting opening on the inside and WAR EMBLEM is making his move." Durkin started counting the furlongs as War Emblem and Medaglia d'Oro dueled on the lead.

We all hit the ceiling, jumping up and down and knowing we were about to see it.

Three furlongs to go!

Then War Emblem crumbled like a used tissue and faded. On the stretch, Sarava kicked it in, battling Medaglia d'Oro for one of the only flashes of brilliance in a pretty lackluster career. Sarava got under it, the biggest upset in the history of the Belmont Stakes: 70-1.

We were dejected, my group of friends, shifting around on our feet and staring at our shoes. It took me a moment to realize that everyone around me wasn't sad. My wife, for some reason, had both hands in the air and a giant smile on her face. What was she doing? She'd flipped!? Had she not just seen the mighty War Emblem, the horse we'd come to see, beaten by a 70-1 no-account nag named . . . and then I remembered that she'd bet him. She was holding a ticket on the biggest upset in Belmont Stakes history.

As I turned to the totalisator to look for her payout and see the results become official, I recalled our conversation forty-five minutes earlier: "I'm going to bet on Sarava. Because my sister's name is Sara, and we're from Virginia." Another friend of mine had piped in and said he was going to bet on Sarava too, because the horse was 70-1, and any horse going off at 70-1 was worth two dollars. (That's not true, if you think about it. Sarava won the 134th Belmont at 70-1, so even in the simplest, nonscientific illustration, the odds of it happening seem to be 134-1. You get odds of only 70-1.)

Still, I figured betting your sister's name on a sunny day while we watched War Emblem slaughter the competition was a fine idea.

"Actually," said my wife, "I think I'll bet an exacta."

"On what?"

"Sarava and Medaglia d'Oro."

"Come on. You don't figure War Emblem to be up there?"

"Just a ten-dollar box on those two. I really like Medaglia d'Oro."

Here's the thing about my wife: she will put money down on her sister's name or a good-looking set of silks, because she's there to have fun and doesn't expect to win any money. But she's good at reading the *Form*. She knows what's what. She's sharp. She can look beyond the Beyer figs and see the running styles. She'll notice preferences for post positions and track condition. She can understand the split fractions. But still— and this is in no way a defense of what I said next—but still, she'd just told me she was betting the longest shot on the board because of my sister-in-law Sara and the state we're from.

"Sweetie, come on."

"Why not?"

"Just give the money to me, why don't you? If you want to throw away twenty dollars on a sucker bet, why don't you just hand it to me and I'll spend it on beer." I said it nicely, as a joke, with a smile on my face, but she's my wife, and I should have been more careful.

Of course I was right in a general sense. I have only one betting maxim, and that is that you stick with what you do. If you go to the window and regularly spend ten dollars, keep doing that; if you play exotics, keep at them. Stay on an even keel and your chances of breaking even are much better than if you chase the pot. If you don't bet exactas, and you don't regularly play the game that way, don't do it. Of course, at the Belmont Stakes, when we're talking about twenty dollars, maxims have nothing to do with it. Rachael wasn't trying to break even.

What were the chances of her hitting that exacta? Pari-mutuel odds don't translate to probability, but it's fair to say that the chances of the 12-8 exacta coming in turned out to be 1227-1. I know that because the two-dollar payout on the exacta was $2,454. I had just cost my wife the bet of a lifetime. I had just cost us $12,000.

This was to be the last betting advice I ever handed my wife. To her eternal credit, she understands the nature of gambling and doesn't hold this woulda coulda shoulda bet against me. Rachael, I apologize.

Disappointment at the Belmont Stakes is nothing new. We are supposed to know better. It's an impossible race.

It's long, for one thing, and the sweeping turns of Belmont's track were designed to make it the "truest" track in the country, meaning that the horse, and not chance or position, rules the outcome.

IN 1894 members of the New York racing community formed the Jockey Club and nominated August Belmont II its leader. He sat at the helm—arguably the most authoritative position in American racing—until his death in 1924. The Jockey Club quickly formed the Westchester Racing Association, with the ironic intent of getting racing out of Westchester and onto Long Island, where the breeders and owners lived along the North Shore.

Belmont and William C. Whitney were especially keen on the plan, and they headed up a syndicate to purchase land for the construction of an elaborate track, one that would suit the aspirations and pretensions of the end-of-the-century wealthy.

They found Elmont (not a foreshortened eponym, it seems) and began purchasing as much land there as they could while keeping their purpose a secret. All through 1902 they bought land, with some of the sellers thinking that a cemetery was to be built, others under the impression the land was to be developed residentially. In September they landed their biggest score when William De Forest Manice sold them his mansion for $125,000. Oatlands, as the mansion was called, was a castle, with turrets and a four-sided tower replete with battlements, a solarium, and peaked windows. (It later operated as the Turf and Field Club until 1956.)

At the end of 1902, the syndicate's purpose became public. It had managed to acquire 650 acres, including the old Hempstead plain where the first races in America were run.

Whitney suggested they name the new track Belmont Park, and the syndicate gathered a workforce that would eventually number one thousand to begin construction. The plan, from day one, was to make this the most elaborate, most ambitious, most luxurious track anyone had seen.

Whitney's death delayed construction, but in 1905 the track opened. Two and a half million dollars had been spent. A clubhouse stood at one end, and a grandstand at the other, with seats on the roof under a striped awning. The paddock was large and shaded by a giant white pine. The pine still stands, now headed toward its two hundredth year.

The real knockout was the track. Most racetracks in America are one mile long; this one was a mile and a half. The turns are sweeping; both stretch runs are long and wide.

On April 10, 1963, the New York Racing Association announced that Belmont Park's grandstand had been deemed unsafe. President James Cox Brady promised to rebuild Belmont as an even bigger, even better track. By November that year it had been torn down, and in 1965 earth was turned on the new Belmont. The track reopened May 20, 1968. It had cost $30.7 million to build. The white pine still stands in the paddock, and the track is still a mile and a half.

The Belmont Stakes, named after the first August Belmont, had been run at Morris Park, and before that at Jerome Park—where it was inaugurated in 1867—but was moved to Belmont in 1905. It is the oldest of the Triple Crown races, and the longest.

On the first Saturday in May, the best three-year-olds in the country run 1-1/4 miles for the first time in the Kentucky Derby. Two weeks later they hit Pimlico and run 1-3/16 around that tight track in the Preakness. Three weeks later they come to the big sandy for the longest dirt race run in America. The schedule is gruesome, and the competition is demanding. (Rock Hard Ten, for instance, had run only three times before arriving in Louisville.) That's why the Triple Crown has been won only eleven times.

Only one of the horses running in the 2004 Preakness, Imperialism, had run as far as American Eclipse and Sir Henry ran when they competed over three four-mile heats in that daylong match race in 1823 at the Union Race Course. It took Imperialism two years to run his twelve miles. Rock Hard Ten's career consisted of three miles of racing. For these fragile thoroughbreds to run a race like the Derby and come back two weeks later in the Preakness is asking a lot. To bring them back three weeks later and send them once around the big oval at Belmont is asking them for all they've got. To win all three races, a horse must be spectacular. The Triple Crown is not a prize won halfheartedly. Seventeen horses had come to Belmont with a chance to do it, and had been unable to pull it off. Another seventeen horses had won the last two legs. Yet another eleven had won the first and last. The list of horses that almost made it all the way is long and illustrious, and it shows how great the short list of the eleven winners really is.

But this was Smarty Jones. He was different somehow, or so it seemed from the headlines: "It's Smarty's Crowning Test," "Elmont Is a One-horse Town," "Smarty Ready to Roll," and my own, the aforementioned "Smarty Will Win by 25 Lengths, Turcotte Vows."

Not just those of us who are easily duped by romanticism but everyone in the racing world seemed to have caught a whiff of this drug, this enthusiasm, this buzz. Smarty was it. This was the thing. Even the consistently cynical Andy Beyer thought Smarty was about to do it.

Driving out to Belmont one morning, I entered the Long Island Expressway by Hunter's Point, in Queens. As I eased my car onto the highway, flashing lights and motorcycles suddenly surrounded me. They had come up fast and seemingly out of nowhere. They whooshed by, traveling at incredible speed, lights turning and flashing, a phalanx of protection. "There goes the motorcade to meet Smarty Jones at the border," I thought.

Three state police departments had rallied police escorts for Smarty's van as he traveled to Belmont from Philadelphia Park, where a public workout had drawn a crowd larger than an average Saturday. A new motorcade would meet him at each state border. The van was chased by helicopters.

The van pulled up to Barn 5 at Belmont, and as Smarty descended the ramp, a wall of photographers ripped off shots as fast as their shutters would click.

Smarty was settled soon enough, and barn manager Bill Foster came out to chat.

"First time I ever had a police escort through three states, I tell you that," Foster said. "People were lined up, waving, hollering. I'm sixty-four, and I've never seen anything like this—you'd have thought the president was coming."

Even after all the photos had been taken and all the interviews wrapped up, no one really wanted to leave Belmont. Even the pros wanted to hang around with Smarty Jones.

Bill Nack was there. He had moved into Barn 5 back when Secretariat was running, and later wrote the best horse racing book I've ever read (*Secretariat: The Making of a Champion*). I asked him how it felt now, whether he wanted to move in again.

"They tore down my tree," he told me. "I used to sit under a tree right over there behind that fence, and it's gone."

I found Robin Smullen, assistant trainer for Funny Cide, lifting linoleum tile off the floor of her office with a putty knife.

"I'm glad it's not us this time. This is really good for racing. It's great to see a horse like this shine. He's an outstanding individual, and in a year like this, with no Alydar to chase him, he really should win it. I hope he does. Have you seen Rock Hard Ten?" She motioned with her hand to indicate that he was very tall. "Everybody wants it to happen, though, you know?"

At the post position draw, Nick Zito—whose horses had run second in the Belmont Stakes five times—said, "Where do I sign up for second? Second to a hero? There's nothing wrong with that."

BELMONT DAY was chilly and grey, with occasional rain. I wandered the facilities among the 120,139 who had come to see history made. The place was swarming. Families, firehouses, and fraternities set up picnics in the huge backyard. GO SMARTY GO hand fans were everywhere.

A friend was in from California, having paid two thousand dollars for two owner's box seats. It was a sterile environment but a welcome respite from the roiling madness going on all around the grounds.

We went to the winner's circle when Wesley Ward's Bear Fan broke a six-furlong record bounding home in an undercard sprint.

A group of my friends, two good old boys from Virginia with their dates, were huddled on the grandstand side at the rail. Some kids from Ohio had the benches behind them, and passed the time doing beer bongs out of a big funnel. A tangle of twenty-something girls slept like a litter of kittens on the concrete.

I stayed by the rail, on the grandstand side. The owner's boxes were too quiet for the race itself. I wanted to feel the ground shake.

The roar of the crowd started during the post parade and continued to swell. Smarty Jones took his place in slot 9. Two and a half minutes until history would be written. We were delirious. We were going to see it happen.

THEY'RE OFF!

Smarty Jones popped out of the gate as if he only had six furlongs ahead of him to cover. He went right to the front. Rock Hard Ten was up there too. Purge, beaten twice in speed duels with Smarty, smashed through on the rail, and that's how they went into the turn.

Around the long first turn, Purge took the lead. Rock Hard Ten was just outside him, running along the second path, all seventeen hands of him pressuring Purge.

Stewart Elliott was trying to settle Smarty Jones along the outside of those two. He was wide all the way around the turn.

Eddington had broken badly, but Jerry Bailey had hustled him up. He'd taken the turn outside of Smarty, already there, already putting pressure on the favorite. Now Bailey had settled him in right behind the three leaders. We'd heard that Eddington was going to bring a new race to the track today, and we knew that Bailey was going to hustle him to the front. He was there, ready to make the move and get into the fray whenever the opportunity arrived.

Behind him, Royal Assault and Birdstone were settled in for the long haul down the backstretch.

They clicked off the quarter-mile in 24-1/5; the half went in 48-3/5. A soft pace, nothing these horses couldn't run.

At the top of the backstretch, Elliott made his move. Smarty Jones took the lead with six furlongs to go. Eddington was putting the pressure on him. "He's not going to get a break today," called Tom Durkin.

Rock Hard Ten was right there.

"Rock Hard Ten looms large, just in behind the lead."

The pace quickened. It was madness. Smarty Jones would push through the third quarter in just over twenty-three seconds—a full second faster than the previous two quarters, and too fast, too early for the long race.

We clenched our smiles. It was hard to tell what was happening on the far side of the track. The call was hard to hear. I saw Smarty take the lead on the big television in the infield, and I didn't like it, but I couldn't judge the pace. The race had started softly. Maybe this was it. Maybe now was when he'd start his pull to the lead, now he'd just open up on these horses, he'd be ten lengths out front going into the turn.

Secretariat had grabbed the lead even earlier, and then let Sham have it while pressuring him. He took it back at the top of the backstretch, poking a head in front, and then slowly just tore it open. Turcotte had said twenty-five lengths. Here we go. Maybe Smarty Jones was the real thing. Maybe this was it.

By the time he'd run three-quarters of a mile, Purge had faded to fourth and was struggling to keep up.

At the five-furlong marker, Rock Hard Ten was on the inside, pressuring. Eddington was on the outside, pressuring. Elliott was having a tough time. The horses were breathing down his neck. He had a bull's-eye painted on his back. They were a minute from the wire, and Smarty Jones was turning it up. He hadn't opened up any daylight, but he was strong on the front.

"Smarty Jones has to hold on to that lead for just one minute more."

Birdstone started to rally around the turn. He had been bred and trained to run like this, to settle in and wait, and then to move. His jockey, Edgar Prado, knew Belmont; he knew it was time to start. He had six lengths to make up.

Purge fell apart on the turn. He was dragging his hooves. He'd end last.

Around the far turn, Smarty Jones let it out another notch. Elliott gave him more head, and the eager three-year-old hero took it. He had a length and a half.

Now Rock Hard Ten fell apart—in the blink of an eye he was three lengths off the lead.

Birdstone ranged up on him and blew by.

Coming into the top of the stretch, Smarty had opened it up to four lengths. Birdstone was a solid second.

This was it.

"AND SMARTY JONES ENTERS THE STRETCH TO THE ROAR OF A HUNDRED AND TWENTY THOUSAND."

I have never felt anything like it: a small city of people cheering, screaming at the top of their lungs, all wanting the same thing. For a glorious moment there was nothing but the chestnut horse and his jock with the blue and white silks. It was a roar of triumph, 120,000 people wanted it to be true, and they shook the foundations of massive Belmont Park.

Then Birdstone hit the stretch. He was coming after him. Smarty would have to earn this.

"THE WHIP IS OUT ON SMARTY JONES. IT'S BEEN TWENTY-SIX YEARS, IT'S JUST ONE FURLONG AWAY!"

And what a furlong it was. Birdstone on the outside, running him down, showing us the first glimpse of what he'd always promised.

But Smarty Jones doesn't lose. Doesn't know how to lose. Elliott had him under the stick. Could he hold on?

They were down to the wire. Birdstone was coming. Smarty was struggling.

"AND BIRDSTONE SURGES!"

Smarty couldn't hold on. Elliott had taken him out and run him fast through those middle quarter-miles—faster than Secretariat had run them, in fact, when he'd clocked twenty-four seconds at each split to set the record that still stands. Smarty had nothing left. The last quarter took almost twenty-seven seconds.

Everyone had thought he was going to make it. Even the jockeys. Javier Castellano, up on Tap Dancer, a horse that never figured, said: "I thought Smarty Jones was going to win

Birdstone, with Edgar Prado up, wins the 136th running of the Belmont Stakes, dashing the Triple Crown hopes of Smarty Jones's followers.

the race from where I was at—about ten lengths behind the field. I told Jose [Santos], turning for home, 'I think he's going to win it.' Then I was surprised to see he didn't."

John Velazquez, the jockey up on Purge, said: "My horse showed up running good today, early on. But he just didn't have enough. When I was coming down the stretch, I was looking at the screen to see what was going on up front. I would have liked to have seen a Triple Crown, but that's how it goes."

John Servis said Smarty Jones didn't settle. Stewart Elliott said Smarty ran a hell of a race. Birdstone just came on like a demon.

Birdstone's owner, Marylou Whitney, could barely hold back her tears as she accepted the trophy. She said, "I'm sorry, I'm sorry, I'm sorry, Smarty Jones."

"I feel a little bad," Birdstone's jockey Edgar Prado said. "I have to do what I have to do—and this is what I get paid for." The man had just won an amazing race, he'd just picked up a $600,000 prize, 10 percent of which was his, and he added: "I feel happy and sad at the same time."

When the veteran turf writer Joe Hirsch retired, he wrote in the *Daily Racing Form*: "What I like most about racing is the high level of competition. When good horses get together, they are capable of putting on a show that is uniquely stirring."

And I'd seen it. Birdstone and Smarty Jones tearing by me, not twenty-five yards away, will remain in my mind forever. Every time I watch the replay, my heart surges as they hit the stretch.

"IT'S BEEN TWENTY-SIX YEARS, IT'S JUST ONE FUR-LONG AWAY!"

That's horse racing. There's always next year.

11
What We've Lost,
What Lies Ahead

W hen I was young, and my grandfather was still alive, we'd go to Hialeah Park, outside of Miami. We'd pull into the long, sweeping driveway, lined by royal palms, in his big, chugging, seventies El Dorado convertible, and cruise up to clubhouse parking. I remember a fountain in which the water had been died a bright blue, though I might have made this up, or it might have been another track. Certainly I found the whole place garish at the time, but I now remember it fondly. Hialeah dripped with habanera decadence, a remnant of some wonderful time before Castro when Havana was a stop for jet-setters.

In the lake in the infield at Hialeah was a flock of pink flamingos. Hialeah was in fact the first place to successfully breed flamingos in captivity. The first chick was born there in 1937 and lived for only two weeks. I think they eventually improved their technique. The flock is still there, as far as I know, and still cared for. I hear the track is still cared for too. The grass is trimmed, the gardens watered, the floor occasionally swept. But no one is there except the skeleton crew responsible for minimal upkeep. The track is dark and has been since 2001—an impotent, aging behemoth, deserted but still groomed.

My grandfather Marty was a sports fan. I have a picture of him standing in a winner's circle somewhere, next to a trotter he owned in part. He's dressed in what looks to be—ridiculous reflection of the flash off of the fabric—a sharkskin suit. A cigarette burns between his fingers. He liked a day at the track and would make reservations at the clubhouse restaurant for dinner. He was king of the silliest bets I've ever known. The best example of the way he gambled, at least in his later years (for all I know he was sharp with the hustle in his middle age) came not at the track but at jai alai.

We were in Tampa, where he lived, watching the game in the reserved section, with plates of margarine-soaked clams oreganato and chewy cuts of something masquerading as prime rib. The smoke of discount-brand cigarettes, bought at the Indian reservation to sidestep taxes, hung heavily in the room like a layer of pungent smog, so thick it gave me the piercing headache that is the calling card of the cigarette hangover. The orange and brown upholstery of the stadium seating was mainly visible: the place was 80 percent empty on a weekend night.

"Max," he told me, "here's some money. Go bet on number 4 to win all day."

"Just number 4? In every game?"

"Do the next few, anyway, and we'll see what happens." He looked at my wife-to-be and said, "Tell you what, make a couple of bets for Rachael too. She can have number 5."

Even if I understood the method by which I might make informed bets at jai alai, handicapping people makes me kind of uncomfortable, unless they are sitting on or training a horse, so I shrugged and placed the bets he wanted.

Marty sat back and watched, happily puffing away. He lost all the bets, though in the paper the next day he saw that number 4 had in fact won the game after we left, the one we hadn't bet on, so he needled me for somehow costing him the score.

Like the Biltmore Hotel, also near Miami, Hialeah was a place that made you want to settle in. The arches of the windows were like a solid bush of ivy, and there were terraces and red-tiled roofs. The stairs out front at the grand entrance were wide and shallow, and cut at right angles off a landing to the big patio. It's a location for movie stars—a location where *everyone* is a movie star. Ava Gardner is supposed to stop on that landing and survey the party before she swishes down to the join the mingling crowd. It's a dark rum kind of place—or it was—a place for lazy afternoons, thin cigars, and slow, steady horseplay.

Joseph Smoot seems to have zipped around the sunnier climes—he was originally from Buffalo—attempting to establish racetracks, all the time running out of money. He was there at the beginning of Hialeah, just as he was briefly in control of Gulfstream and Santa Anita. Hialeah began as a real estate gamble. James H. Bright bought hundreds of acres of swampland and used much of it for pasture. A dog track and a jai-alai fronton were built on the land, and they were success-ful. So Bright and Smoot started a racetrack. They managed to open the track and even held a few seasons of racing in the mosquito-infested, snake-filled marshes of the Florida coun-tryside, but the depression hit the venture hard. It was sold off and ended up in Joseph Widener's hands.

Do a search of the National Gallery collection by prove-nance and you'll turn up more than three hundred pieces that were given to the gallery by Widener, in his father Peter's name. The Widener Collection, along with the Mellon Collection, is the cornerstone of that great museum and consists of every-thing from Corot to antique Chinese vases, Rembrandt to De-gas. In what has become, at least in this context, an almost banal fantasy of the very rich, Widener had a vision for Hialeah. He wanted to make it the most luxurious, beautiful venue any-one had ever seen. He imported birds from around the world, he landscaped, and he hired Lester Geisler to design the track.

The design was a knockout. The back of the grandstand was enclosed with a lattice of cypress, the bridal path lined with towering Australian pines, puffy and tall. The statue of the great Citation stood in a basin covered with lily pads.

Like everywhere that horsemen enjoy spending their time, it was said that horses liked Hialeah. Citation certainly liked it, as did Northern Dancer, War Admiral, Spectacular Bid, and Seattle Slew. Buckpasser ran his "Chicken Flamingo" here, when the odds were so prohibitive that Hialeah called off bet-ting on the race.

From 1947 until 1971, Hialeah had a state-mandated control of winter racing dates. In the early seventies this control began to slip. First, the mandate that awarded winter racing to Hialeah was overturned. Then the track was sold twice and ended up in John Brunetti's hands.

In its last decades, Hialeah saw an incredible decline in attendance. The building began to crumble. The track had gone broke in 1976, allowing Brunetti's purchase. In 1989, Florida racing was deregulated, and Hialeah was forced to compete with other tracks. The handle dwindled, no one came, and it shut down.

Andy Beyer wrote in the *Washington Post*:

> Hialeah's principal problem can be summed up in one word: demographics. The track that was once at the center of American racing finds itself far removed from the affluent northern communities to which tourists flock; it sits in an inelegant neighborhood. Gulfstream Park and Calder Race Course are much better situated to lure the sport's prime customers.

Brunetti had some clout. He swung into action and got the track back on its feet. But he couldn't rely on his connections forever. By 2001 he had lost his allies. Gulfstream and Calder had all the dates. Hialeah was closed.

THE OPENING of Pimlico can be traced to 1868, when things were starting to cook at Saratoga and Milton Sanford threw a dinner party. He had won the Saratoga Cup with Lancaster. The meet was going incredibly well. Drunk on Saratoga water, high on the success so evident all around them, the men at the party decided to make a stakes race called "The Dinner Party

Stakes." Oden Bowie, the governor of Maryland who had made money selling blankets during the Civil War, chucked in fifteen thousand dollars for the purse—a staggering sum at the time. They would run the race in two years to commemorate the fun they were having, and it would be for horses that were yearlings at the time.

The Maryland Jockey Club was nothing new. George Washington had lost money at the races in Maryland, and Andrew Jackson was an honorary member. But there was no track in Baltimore until the club turned its attention to getting one built to host the Dinner Party Stakes.

The location the club found was a spot lovingly referred to as Old Hilltop. The area around the seventy acres purchased by the Maryland Jockey Club was known as Pimlico. Apparently the original English settlers of the vicinity were from London and missed their pub: Old Ben Pimlico's Tavern.

The track was completed in time for the race. It was a mile oval that circled the hill in the infield. The hill provided excellent viewing, and the infield was clogged with carriages on opening day, a balmy October 25, 1870.

It was a great success. Two days later the horn blew the call to the post for the Dinner Party Stakes. Earlier they had run the Breakfast Stakes and the Supper Stakes, but the Dinner Party Stakes was the big event—the promise made over dinner had become a reality. Edward Hotaling wrote that "Sanford himself entered a Lexington colt—he was so ungainly they labeled him a cart horse—and won that improbable Dinner Party Stakes. Three years hence, Pimlico's first hero would become immortal by lending his name to another race there, the Preakness."

The gingerbread members' clubhouse at Pimlico.

Pimlico weathered the racing ban of 1910 by installing pari-mutuel machines, which were deemed less of a sin than the crooked bookmaking operations that had dominated betting. Well-heeled Baltimoreians relaxed in the opulent luxury of the members' clubhouse, built for the opening in 1870, with a wraparound balcony, what looks like a thousand windows, and enough gingerbread to float a Victorian ocean liner. Originally, the cupola was graced by a weather vane shaped like an arrow. When it was struck by lightning in 1909, it was replaced with an iron weather vane in the shape of a horse and rider, painted in the colors worn by the jock up on the winner of the 1909 Preakness, a horse named Effendi. When the members' club-house burned down in 1966, all that was saved was the weather vane. They didn't want to take a chance with that one, so they put it in the little Pimlico museum and built a replica in the infield, atop a model of the clubhouse cupola. Each year the weather vane is painted the colors of the winner of the Preakness, moments after the race.

I've always encountered a strange atmosphere of phoniness around Pimlico. Black-eyed Susans are the flowers that are won at the Preakness, but they're not in season when the race is run, so they obsessively paint white and yellow daisies by the thousands to resemble them. The weather vane is a replica. I'm happy that the real weather vane is there, and I'm happy it's being preserved. I just always feel a little put on. Over the years, though, the racing has been anything but a put-on.

Pimlico, for instance, is the site of the only time the House of Representatives was adjourned to watch a race. It was 1877, and the big race was between Parole, Ten Broeck, and Tom Ochiltree. Ten Broeck won and set a new record for four miles.

But my favorite piece of history, out of many fantastic races run at Pimlico over the years, came in the spring of 1920, when Sam Riddle's silks were painted on the famed weather vane. If Riddle had liked racing in Kentucky, and thought that three-year-olds were capable of running ten furlongs, Man o' War would no doubt have won the Triple Crown.

Man o' War was born March 29 (also my birthday) in 1917. He looked leggy and spindly as a yearling and was sold at Saratoga for five thousand dollars. By the time he was two, there was no mistaking Big Red. He was beaten only once, in the Sanford Memorial at Saratoga as a two-year-old. When the flag was dropped to run in that race—there were no electric gates in 1919—Man o' War wasn't even facing in the right direction. The race was only six furlongs. It can't exactly be said that Man o' War got off badly; once he started, he ran well. But he certainly gave everybody else a head start.

Johnny Loftus was up in the irons, and he and Man o' War shot up to the field, quickly passing all but the quickest two-year-olds out that day. Loftus went to the inside to save ground, and was boxed in. Donnacona was on the inside, and fading. Loftus had to check Man o' War and take him to the outside. Golden Broom was leading, but he was struggling under the weight assigned him. Upset was challenging him, shook him, and took off down the stretch.

Man o' War was swinging closed behind Upset. He was gaining on Upset all down the stretch, but there wasn't enough track. Upset had him by half a length at the wire. The only horse to ever beat Big Red had needed a head start and a horrible trip around the track. They'd meet six times, and Upset never got close again.

Man o' War blasted through the rest of his two-year-old season. He came out of a winter's rest weighing a strong 1,150 pounds, standing tall. No prodigy resting on his two-year-old laurels, Big Red was going to be even more indomitable as a three-year-old. He set about proving it immediately.

The Preakness was the fourth race on the card in its thirteenth year, with a value of $25,000 plus the nomination fees, $23,000 of which went to whichever horse was in front after a mile and an eighth. They spent six minutes goofing around at the post, and were off at 4:14 P.M. On the seventh path, Man o' War wasted no time at all getting to that first turn. He popped to the front and blazed around Pimlico's tight oval. With only a quarter of a mile run, he already had a two-length advantage. King Thrush was trying to chase him and was second in the wake of what the *Racing Form* chart refers to as Man o' War's "terrific pace." He ran the first quarter in 23-2/5, and the half in 47-3/5. More impressively, he kept it up. He ran six furlongs, where King Thrush was "killed off" in 1:12-2/5. He covered the next quarter-mile in 25-4/5. Upset was on his way, under heavy punishment, but "resolute." He was no match, Man o' War had "abundant" speed in reserve, plenty of gas in the tank. He peeled off the final furlong in 13-2/5, coasting to the finish a length and a half in front.

Big Red was back, and it looked like he wasn't even trying.

For years Alfred G. Vanderbilt was president of the Maryland Jockey Club. He staged the incredible battle between Seabiscuit and Big Red's son War Admiral at Pimlico. (It was a *grand* track.) In their media guide (the fellow who found it for me said, "We get so few requests . . .") Vanderbilt declares: "Pimlico is more than a dirt track bounded by four streets. It is an accepted American institution, devoted to the best interests of a great sport, graced by time, respected for its honorable past."

It's hard to believe he's talking about the same place. Pimlico today is an unhappy, run-down track. Yet because of some trick of the way it's built, it still offers some of the most intimate racing I've ever seen. Even up in the dining room you seem closer to the track than anywhere I've been. On the rail you feel practically in the race.

Part of that feeling comes from the fact that there are so few people around you could hear a pin drop. When the horses hit the stretch, the two guys who are yelling them home are pretty far away from you, and you can hear the jockeys whooping and the snap of the sticks on the thoroughbred flanks.

People go to Pimlico once a year, for the Preakness, and it's ignored for the rest of the season.

I visited Pimlico on Breeders' Cup day 2004. The Breeders' Cup was being run in Texas, but a day like that usually brings a few folks to the betting windows. I've seen Upper West Side moms brave the OTB on Breeders' Cup day. They don't make eye contact, they try not to touch anything, but they're in there, putting their two-dollar bets down. (More likely their string of two-hundred-dollar exotics. A lot of people gamble more than we think—in fact, Mom is probably there every day, it was me who was the weekender.)

Pimlico, however, was deserted. Old men sat at the simulcast screens in batches of six. They were nice guys, but they are not about to keep the place alive.

It was grim, grey, and dirty.

The racing product at Pimlico, as one might unromantically call the day-to-day allowance and claiming races run at most tracks throughout the country, has historically been very good. It can boast a thriving state breeding program, attractive purses, and good surfaces on which to run. Good enough to attract racing giant Magna to the deal table a few years ago. Magna Entertainment had been spun out of its parent company, Magna International, an automotive parts supplier founded in 1999 by Frank Stronach. The Magna mission, or promise, is to invigorate racing by turning tracks into entertainment centers. Magna operates or manages eleven thor-

Pimlico on a Saturday: the thrill is gone.

oughbred racetracks as well as some harness racing tracks, an Austrian "racino," simulcasting and off-track betting venues, an online account wagering service, and a television channel called HorseRacing TV.

Andy Beyer wrote in the *Washington Post* on April 13, 2004:

Magna's president, Frank Stronach, had good intentions and high hopes when his company purchased the Maryland tracks in July 2002; the price tag will be $117 million when Magna buys out the remaining interests of Joe and Karin De Francis. Businesses making investments of this magnitude are usually welcomed in a state, and Magna officials were surely stunned by the rude reception they got during the slot debate. After Gov. Robert L. Ehrlich Jr. proposed installing slot machines in the state's tracks, opponents railed against the "greedy track owners" who would stand to benefit. Even Ehrlich eventually floated the un-Republican idea of having the state take over racing by building a track in downtown Baltimore and running the Preakness there.

Throughout the debate, few politicians displayed concern for the health of the horse business. Michael Busch, the House speaker who was largely responsible for killing slots, put it bluntly: "I think the amount of people who care [about horse racing] is next to none." The industry failed to win its argument that the horse business is so vital to the Maryland economy that it deserves some help.

In October 2004, Beyer wrote:

I have been following the races in Maryland since the mid-1960s, and I have never seen the quality of racing lower than it has been at Pimlico in the last few months. The reason is simple: Purses in Maryland have fallen far behind those in neighboring states that receive an infusion of slot money. Without slots of its own, Maryland has no hope of catching up.

Beyer suggested that there might be real consequences to alienating Pimlico, namely that Magna could—and should—move the Preakness to Santa Anita.

AS OF this writing, Magna has torn down the old Gulfstream Park in Florida. This season's racing will be run on a new track in a bizarre country-fair setting of tents and jumbotrons. They will build an entertainment center, a real lollapalooza. From the descriptions it sounds very Vegas. The new place won't be ready until 2006. Opening day of the interim setting was troubled with not nearly enough tellers, a very confusing layout, and a difficult time getting a view of the races. Magna found another jumbotron and brought it in.

Here's Bill Finley in the *New York Times*:

> The end result is expected to be a palatial racetrack, perhaps like nothing anyone has ever seen. The Gulfstream Park of the future will include a dazzling new clubhouse, a lush one-mile turf course, state-of-the-art barns, a poker room, condos, shops, a movie theater and a hotel. It's getting to that point that is the problem.

The basic idea is that racing is not getting any more popular, so why not surround it with things that are popular, like shopping and movies, and see if you can catch a few bucks off the foot traffic?

Gulfstream opened in 1939 in Hallandale, Florida, just around the time Meyer Lansky arrived. Lansky, for all his reputation as the Brain behind it all, was basically a gambler. He made his money by organizing games for bettors.

Florida had boomed in the 1920s. Real estate development was a gold mine. But the one-two punch of the 1926 hurricane, which left much of southern Florida in ruin, and the 1927 stock market crash and subsequent depression, reverted Florida to an almost wild state, what Robert Lacey referred to in his book on Meyer Lansky as a backwoods country. "Palm Beach and Miami derived some brief winter comfort from those visitors rich enough to keep up the traditions of the January-to-March season. But these were rare islands in a sea of mosquitos and sand fleas."

Hallandale was across the line, Lacey explains, part of an American tradition of havens for vice sitting just outside of a city. Bergen County, New Jersey; Jefferson Parish, Louisiana—everywhere in the country there was a place across the river, across the county line, where the cops would play along and the carpet joints would rake it in.

> The "city" of Hallandale was an impoverished farming community of a few hundred families, situated on the southern border of Broward County, halfway between Miami and Fort Lauderdale. Hallandale's only visitors during the season were the "fruit tramps"—itinerant pickers who arrived for the tomato harvest every spring, and who shacked up, for a dollar a night, in a fly-blown local rooming house, the Collins Hotel.
>
> But the no-man's-land location of Hallendale proved the secret of its success. Desperate for income of any sort, its inhabitants were as willing to bend the law as were the inhabitants of other across-the-line corners of America.

Meyer Lansky and Lucky Luciano, founder of Murder, Inc., didn't start the gambling joints in Hallandale, but they quickly insinuated themselves and expanded the business. The dog track opened, and then Gulfstream Park. It was heaven, a gamblers' dream, loud, bawdy, and open.

In his *Mafia Encyclopedia*, Carl Sifakis wrote that the area around Hallandale and Gulfstream Park is still referred to by many residents as "Lanskyland." It's difficult to get any real information about the Mafia's connection to horse racing. Al Rothstein openly owned the Red Stone Stable, about as close to running the horses under your own name as you can get, but most of the connections work along the lines of knowing a guy who knows a guy who heard about a guy who knew about a thing. Vague.

Joseph Smoot started Gulfstream, and again he ran out of money. This time he seems to have simply walked off the scene after turning ownership over to the contractor, John C. Horning, who had been hired to build the park.

Despite the Hallandale hotbed, Gulfstream had a difficult time competing with Hialeah, and the battle for Florida racing dates began almost immediately. I think it surprised many folks that Gulfstream won this battle in the end. It certainly didn't look like it would win anything when Horning declared bankruptcy and closed the place in 1939, the same year it opened.

A well-connected florist named James Donn bought it in 1944.

Someone did once say of Donn, "Yeah, a florist. . . ." I have little idea what that means, but the landscaping at Gulfstream did improve markedly. He planted hundreds of palms and flowers. For the longest time a Mississippi riverboat, in miniature, would paddle around the infield lake, which was filled with alligators. I have spent a few dreamy moments hoping for an alligator attack on the riverboat.

All of it now is gone, except the *Suwannee Queen*. They've saved the riverboat, and they intend to drop it back into the infield lake (though when I called to ask after it, they offered to sell it to me).

Gulfstream was an oasis of old Florida in what has become an increasingly mundane sea of developer's fantasies. The old poured concrete, the boomerang "modern" signage, the pastels—all signaled a slightly weathered but fully authentic Florida. Neighborhoods such as Coral Gables and Coconut Grove will always be more appealing than the green-glassed monsters that have shot up along the beach. Florida as "Florida," that is, Florida as a narcissistic theme park, operating at a remove, will be a husk.

It might work. I have no idea what most people want. But I know that developers have destroyed incredible swaths of the East Coast, from New Jersey to the Eastern Shore of Maryland, from Loudoun County, Virginia, to North Carolina. What typifies most of the development is a lack of imagination: the beige house rules. Each place once offered unique aesthetic satisfactions, but when all the coast is corporatized, aesthetic concerns will be entertained only as a subset of pecuniary interests.

I have no idea whether people who do not like horse racing will want to go to the track to see a movie or buy some khakis. I have a pretty good idea that the core racing fan does not need access to a jewelry shop—except maybe on a very good day. Will a shopping mall and some condos save horse racing? Can we rely on income from slots?

I know as many people who claim that racing is healthier than ever as I do folks who think we're done for. Certainly there is no lack of action; the gambling dollar is rolling around like a freight train. There is always a temptation to forecast the future of racing, but things change so quickly, and the forces at work are so myriad and bureaucratic, that I can't possibly pretend to have a handle on it.

Horse racing people say, "Well, so what, so we're left with Del Mar, Keeneland, and Saratoga. Those are the only places you want to be anyway." I have heard this said by track presidents, OTB staffers, and librarians. I have even said it myself.

But as I've tried to demonstrate in this book, the best stories happen all over the place. They happen at Del Mar, Keeneland, and Saratoga, yes, but they happen at Pimlico and Aqueduct too. The truth is, they happen at Evangeline in Louisiana and at Charles Town in West Virginia. When I think about Joe Hirsch's "uniquely stirring" competition, I can't help but realize that it's going on every day, all year long.

I hope that Magna's big Gulfstream gamble pays off. Above all I hope we can see a way through the bureaucracies to keep racing alive. The successful tracks have proved that racing can put people in the seats. How we maintain that success around the country, I don't know. But I've got my fingers crossed.

And I'm on my way to Aqueduct. I feel lucky.

Index

Index

Index

Index

A NOTE ON THE AUTHOR

Max Watman is the regular turf correspondent for the *New York Sun* and has written about horse racing for the *New York Times* and New York City Off-Track Betting. His work has also appeared in the *Wall Street Journal* and *Parnassus*. Mr. Watman is also the fiction chronicler for *The New Criterion* and an editor of the *Nebraska Review*. He was born in Washington, D.C., grew up in the mountains of Virginia, and now lives with his wife in Cold Spring, New York.